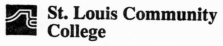

TRASH CULTURE

TRASH CULTURE

POPULAR CULTURE
AND THE GREAT TRADITION

Richard Keller Simon

UNIVERSITY OF CALIFORNIA PRESS

Berkeley   Los Angeles   London

University of California Press
Berkeley and Los Angeles, California

University of California Press, Ltd.
London, England

© 1999 by the Regents of the University of California

Library of Congress Cataloging-in-Publication Data

Simon, Richard Keller.
    Trash culture : popular culture and the great tradition /
Richard Keller Simon.
        p.   cm.
    Includes bibliographical references and index.
    ISBN 0-520-21647-4 (alk. paper).—ISBN 0-520-22223-7
(alk. paper)
        1. Popular culture—United States.   2. United States—
Civilization—1970–   3. United States—Civilization—
European influences.   4. Influence (Literary, artistic, etc.)
5. Storytelling—Social aspects—United States.   I. Title.
E169.12.S5186   1999
306.4'0973—dc21   99-21164
                                                                    CIP

Manufactured in the United States of America

08 07 06 05 04 03 02 01 00 99   10 9 8 7 6 5 4 3 2 1

The paper used in this publication meets the minimum
requirements of ANSI/NISO Z39.48-1992 (R 1997)
(*Permanence of Paper*).

For
Rhoda Simon
Kathy Waddell
Noah Simon-Waddell

In loving memory
Israel Simon
Hermina Keller Weitzenfeld

Contents

Acknowledgments

I could not have written this book without the assistance and inspiration of a number of talented and patient people. At the University of California, San Diego, Dwight Macdonald and Ursula LeGuin lectured in the very first courses I offered on popular culture, Stanley Aronowitz introduced me to the work of Horkheimer and Adorno, and NBC News televised me giving a lecture on advertising and literature. It was a dramatic beginning. Over the course of many quieter years at the University of Texas at Austin I benefited from discussions about popular culture with Roger Abrahams, Tony Hilfer, Douglas Kellner, and Horace Newcomb. More recently, many of my students at California Polytechnic State University in San Luis Obispo have written papers about the subjects treated in this book, and some of their ideas and perceptions are incorporated in what follows. Stephen Wyman allowed me to watch a series of rehearsals of the television soap opera *Days of Our Lives* and agreed to an interview about the differences between directing in the theater and in television. Jim Magnuson talked to me about the challenges of writing for the television serial *Knots Landing* and arranged for me to meet members of the cast and crew and watch an afternoon of filming. Michael Curtis came to my class to talk about his experiences as a writer for *Friends*. Steve Coffman, Katie Gittes, Tony Hilfer, Steve Marx, Horace Newcomb, Wayne Rebhorn, Robert Thompson, James Twitchell, and Mike Wenzl have evaluated all or parts of the book.

At the University of California Press, Linda Norton has nurtured this project from the beginning, providing valuable advice, direction, and encouragement as I worked through a series of rewrites and revisions. She has been a wonderful editor. Her assistant, Chris Robyn, was always available to answer my questions. Madeleine Adams edited my copy with grace and precision, Julie Christianson worked effectively to test-market the manuscript, and Mary Severance oversaw the entire production process with patience and skill.

California Polytechnic State University has supported this project by awarding me released time, summer fellowships, and a sabbatical leave. My wife, Kathy Waddell, has supported this project with her love, patience, and understanding, and our son, Noah Eric Simon-Waddell, has supported it by asking me to explain my ideas to him, by watching television programs and movies with me about which I was writing, and by coming to my classroom to demonstrate his favorite video games when he was in elementary school. My parents, Rhoda and Si Simon, read and critiqued an early version of this book, just as long before they had guided my experiences with television, the movies, and literature. This book is dedicated to them, and to my maternal grandmother, Hermina Keller Weitzenfeld, who taught English for many years at South Philadelphia High School, and in whose steps I follow.

Earlier versions of three chapters have been published previously: "Advertising as Literature: The Utopian Fiction of the American Marketplace" in *Texas Studies in Literature and Language* 22 (summer 1980), reprinted by permission of the University of Texas Press; "Euripides and the *Enquirer*" in *Genre* 24 (spring 1991), copyright University of Oklahoma; and "The Formal Garden in the Age of Consumer Culture" in *Mapping American Culture*, edited by Wayne Franklin and Michael Steiner, Iowa City: University of Iowa Press, 1992, copyright University of Iowa.

CHAPTER 1

Trash and Literature

The stories that surround us in our daily lives are very similar to the great literature of the past. If you watch television, go to the movies, read popular magazines, and look at advertisements you are exposed to many of the same kinds of stories as someone who studies the great books of Western civilization. You have simply been encouraged to look at them differently. A tabloid newspaper such as *The National Enquirer* is a fragmented version of great dramatic tragedy—Euripides, Ibsen, or Strindberg made into celebrity gossip and sold at supermarket checkout counters next to the candy bars and the gum. The suffering and fall of the ancient nobility is now the suffering and fall of aging movie stars, and although they do not speak in the same dramatic language, they suffer and fall, and even learn about themselves, in much the same fashion. Similarly, the movie *Rambo: First Blood, Part II* is a contemporary variation on Homer's *Iliad*, with the long and horrible war in Vietnam in place of the long and horrible war in Troy, and a muscle-bound Sylvester Stallone playing a contemporary version of Achilles. *Star Trek* contains many of the same basic plot lines, character types, and overall thematic concerns of *Gulliver's Travels*, and although little of Jonathan Swift's harsh satire remains, new political realities are obviously in place: A whole team of heavily armed space voyagers now polices the universe in place of the lone and misanthropic Gulliver. *Cosmopolitan* is a glitzy, commercialized reworking of the central concerns of some of the great women's coming-of-age novels of the last two hundred years, the successor to works such as *Sense and Sensibility, Madame Bovary*, and *The House of Mirth*. The problems faced by Elinor and Marianne Dashwood, Emma Bovary, and Lily Bart are the great subjects of the magazine.

All of this may be either good or bad, revolting or reassuring, depending on your tastes in literature, but the relationship between great books and popular entertainment is important and worth examining carefully. What really is the difference between trash culture and the great tradition? Why is *The National Enquirer* so bad and a tragedy by Euripides so good? For people with inquiring minds but short attention spans, our stories of suffering, fall, and recognition now come in short, easy-to-read fragments as a kind of fast-food tragedy-to-go, but the fragments themselves contain nearly all of the essential elements of dramatic tragedy. Do we demand completeness, a beginning, middle, and end, as Aristotle insisted twenty-five hundred years ago? Do we require a single author, intentionally creating the story? Some of the great avant-garde artists of the early twentieth century have ripped the art of the past into fragments, more recent apostles of postmodernism have lectured us about the fragmentary nature of experience, and some of our most distinguished cultural critics have argued that authors are irrelevant. If they are right, we ought to hail the *Enquirer* as ancient literature reworked according to the principles of the new and *Cosmopolitan* as a courtship novel subjected to this same kind of avant-garde revisionism. Or is this shift from Euripides to the *Enquirer*, from the novels of Jane Austen, Gustave Flaubert, and Edith Wharton to *Cosmopolitan*, just another sign of the decay of Western civilization?

Many of the differences between trash culture and high culture show only that storytelling adapts to changing economic, social, and political conditions. Sylvester Stallone is not a great actor, but the part he plays in *Rambo* is a diminished, inarticulate version of Achilles, for which his skills are quite appropriate. One of the major points of the movie is that military heroism is completely out of place in our world, and thus Stallone's character must appear lame, perhaps even lamer than he intended. If the shift from *The Iliad* to *Rambo* is to be taken as a sign of the decline of Western civilization, it is not the fault of the storytellers, who are only remaking the epic for new anti-epic realities. Similarly, Swift could only have written *Star Trek* if he had been on antidepressants (*Prozac* would be a great name for a *Star Trek* character), but Gene Roddenberry's upbeat version of the fantastic journey story form has been wildly successful on television and in the movies, where audiences clearly prefer hope to despair, earnestness to satire. Does *Star Trek* tell us what we want to hear while *Gulliver's Travels* delivers what we need to hear? Perhaps. But it is also worth remembering that Swift wrote his savage denunciation of humanity in an age of optimism, but Roddenberry and his teams of writers deliver their message of hope in a far more despairing age. *Star Trek* may therefore be just as appropriate for us as *Gulliver's Travels* was for Swift's first readers.

In a similar fashion, the woman on the cover of *Cosmopolitan* may be a horribly sexist stereotype, but she can also be seen as Emma Bovary's younger, much more successful sister. Indeed, if Madame Bovary had only subscribed to *Cosmo* she would be alive and well today, so closely are her concerns addressed by the magazine. And wouldn't she be better off alive and happy? Or do we still insist that women who look for sexual satisfaction outside of marriage end up dead? Emma Bovary seeks happiness in materialism and in eroticism, risking everything in extramarital affairs, and then dies because of her behavior. The *Cosmo* woman seeks the same pleasures but avoids Emma's fate.

Cosmopolitan is not the same as *Madame Bovary* by any means, but it is very similar not only in its overall thematic preoccupations, but also in many of its specific story lines, plot conflicts, and character types. The same is true of the other pairings with which this book is concerned. The contemporary American shopping mall reworks many of the standard elements of the great European formal garden from the Middle Ages to the eighteenth century, adapting its statues, vistas, pathways, walls, and objects for enjoyment and contemplation to new commercial purposes. *Playboy* addresses many of the same problems as Baldazar Castiglione's *Book of the Courtier*, the great courtesy book of the Italian Renaissance, and proposes many of the same solutions. Plot lines and character types from the television soap opera *Days of Our Lives* are very similar to some of the great Jacobean revenge tragedies of the English Renaissance. The connections between high and low are extensive and systematic, and one of the purposes of this book is to demonstrate that trash culture replicates *all* of the major genres of literature. We are surrounded by stories that echo, repeat, revise, and adapt the entire history of literature, something that is not only exciting in its own right, but also important for our understanding of literature, both high and low. All past literature, T. S. Eliot argues in "Tradition and the Individual Talent," is simultaneously present and available to us. In its contemporary variants, it is also the cultural environment in which we live.

In part, this is because writers for television and the movies imitate the classics, often in careful and meticulous detail, just as writers of poetry, drama, and the novel have always done. Sometimes they make this explicit, as Francis Ford Coppola does in *Apocalypse Now*, his remake of Joseph Conrad's *Heart of Darkness*, or Amy Heckerling does in *Clueless,* her remake of Jane Austen's *Emma*. But more often than not we are offered no indication that a particular television program or movie reworks an earlier work of literature except for the details of the story itself. Virtually everything that happens in the Jim Carey movie *Dumb and Dumber*, for example, repeats Cervantes's *Don Quixote*, from the basic concept of two really dumb goofs who go on the road to serve a beautiful woman, to the most important details of character and plot: that one is a confused idealist and the other, his sidekick, is a not-too-bright realist; that they ride in a van decked out to look like a shaggy animal; that they seek a woman who wants to have nothing to do with them; that they endure a series of comic pratfalls and misadventures, including a good number of toilet and bodily function jokes; and, in the central fantasy of the story, that they imagine the idealist pulling the heart out of a hated rival. *Dumb and Dumber* is a film version of *Don Quixote* for kids.

But not all of the similarities between contemporary entertainment and the great tradition can be explained as conscious imitation. Novels such as *Sense and Sensibility, Madame Bovary*, and *The House of Mirth* are similar to *Cosmopolitan* not because the editors of the magazine are avid readers of these novels (although that is possible), but because all of these writers and editors struggle with a common subject, the predicament of women in courtship, and all of them wish to appeal to readers with certain needs and interests. Austen, Flaubert, and Wharton, working through a real problem faced by real women of a certain age and class, and the editors of *Cosmopolitan*, working through a similar problem faced by women of a similar age and class, come up with similar stories. This should not be surprising. *Playboy* and *The Book of the Courtier* are similar not because the editors of the magazine read Castiglione, but because both set about writing manuals for men on the brink of adulthood about the best ways of being a man, and both devote a great deal of attention to the best methods of seducing women. The needs of young men in sixteenth-century Italy and in contemporary America turn out to be remarkably similar, in many respects identical. And the needs of the audience clearly determine, at least in part, the nature of these works. Supermarket tabloids such as the *Enquirer* fill a need for stories about the suffering and fall of the rich and famous that was previously satisfied by the writers of dramatic tragedy.

Of course, this does not make them equal to each other in terms of language, characterization, and plot. But very few people attend productions of Greek tragedies these days, and even in fifth-century B.C. Athens, tragedies were only presented once or twice a year. By contrast, the *Enquirer* makes a great wealth of tragic stories available every week at very little cost and claims "the largest circulation of any paper in America." Brevity, clarity, and accessibility are the principles of this new tragic form, and if dramatic tragedy is now reduced to its most fundamental elements, who is to say that this is necessarily bad? We know that a tabloid newspaper is tawdry entertainment and a Greek tragedy is great literature, of course, even if both deal with the same basic kinds of material, because one appeals to large numbers of people and the other to a small educated elite. This is a very old bias that has been hard for critics to move beyond. After all, we learn in school that literature is something that we must read very carefully (usually because we will be tested on it), and trash culture is escapist entertainment, rarely worth thinking about for very long. If our appreciation of Greek tragedy is a sign of our membership in the elect, then our interest in the *Enquirer* is a sign of our depravity and lack of education. What we miss is the opportunity to understand the similarities between trash culture and the great tradition.

Our bias against popular storytelling prevents us from considering it as carefully as we consider great literature because it effectively cuts trash culture off from the tradition of literature that critics have historically valued. It is against that tradition that we almost always read and evaluate stories, at least the stories that our teachers have asked us to study, respect, and interpret, but we evaluate popular entertainment against various nonliterary traditions, against newspapers, for example, or against a concept of mass entertainment that we assume means simple content that is not worth the trouble of examining carefully. E. D. Hirsch puts it this way: "An interpreter's preliminary generic conception of a text is constitutive of everything that he subsequently understands and . . . this remains the case unless and until that generic conception is altered" (*Validity*, 74). In other words, we find what we expect to find.

We evaluate the *Enquirer* as a tawdry kind of newspaper because of its superficial resemblances to a newspaper, even though it is hardly filled with traditional news, and we dismiss it as trash because so much of its celebrity gossip is false or exaggerated. But when we evaluate the *Enquirer* against the tradition of made-up stories of suffering, fall, and self-recognition, its stories are immediately identifiable as tragedy in an age when tragedy is supposed to have died, transformations of one of the oldest and most beloved genres of literature into something lively and widely accessible. The *Enquirer* becomes quite interesting because we are reading the tragedy of our own time, and that calls for an attention to detail, a care with the text, that we would never have brought to a trashy newspaper. Nothing about the *Enquirer* has changed, only our attitude toward it.

Similarly, we identify *Rambo* as a typical, violent action-adventure story, and because it is full of gun battles, stars a muscle-bound Sylvester Stallone, and has one-dimensional characters we dismiss it as mindless entertainment or, worse yet, as propaganda because it makes no secret of its political stance toward the war in Vietnam. But when we evaluate *Rambo* against the tradition of stories of long, grim, but sometimes heroic warfare, it turns out to be very similar to the *Iliad*, the first great Western epic, now made accessible, even quite compelling, to millions of moviegoers. Immediately *Rambo* becomes much more interesting, no longer only mindless entertainment or propaganda, but evidence of changes in the epic form as we have tried to make sense of our own war. Achilles is at the very top of the social hierarchy in *The Iliad*, wealthy, respected, and articulate, but Stallone's character, John Rambo, is at the very bottom of the social hierarchy in *Rambo*, poor, scorned, and inarticulate. They face almost identical problems in almost identical situations but from opposite positions of power. *Rambo* is *The Iliad* adapted to new conditions, a story no longer for a small warrior aristocracy but for a large war-making democracy. *The Iliad* retains its great strength as a story for contemporary American movie audiences, even in greatly changed circumstances. The differences between *Rambo* and *The Iliad* reflect the differences between our own civilization and that of ancient Greece; the other pairs with which this book is concerned also refract universal human themes through different cultural prisms. John Rambo's powerlessness and his sense of futility, the loud sexuality and materialism of *Cosmopolitan*, the fragmentation and sensationalism of the stories in the *Enquirer*, and the upbeat cooperative ethic of *Star Trek* are all characteristics of current consumer society in the West, and thus are appropriate developments in the literary tradition.

"The uniqueness of a work of art is inseparable from its being imbedded in the fabric of tradition," Walter Benjamin writes in "The Work of Art in the Age of Mechanical Reproduction" (223). But in popular art, Benjamin argues, "the technique of reproduction detaches the reproduced object from the domain of tradition" (221). Benjamin himself liked the idea of a popular art freed from its tradition because of the possibilities it held out for new political functions, but what he wished for a half century ago has not come to pass. Instead of liberated political art, we are faced with movies, television programs, advertisements, and other forms of trash or popular culture that effectively mask their traditions from us, thereby obscuring their meanings. The solution to this problem lies in using Benjamin's insight but in reversing the process. Thus, this book returns such mechanically and/or electronically reproduced popular stories back into the tradition of storytelling so that they can be more clearly understood.

Teaching Popular Culture and the Great Tradition

For most of the last thirty years I have taught courses in literature and popular culture at a number of different American universities. This book is the result of what I have learned from colleagues, students, and the stories themselves as I have moved back and forth between high and low. I have written it for an audience of students, colleagues, and readers outside of the university who I hope will be interested in what I have to say here: that the history of storytelling is full of rich and exciting connections between high and low.

I began in the late 1960s by linking rock and roll to poetry, hoping thereby to lead students from the lyrics they loved to the lyrics I wanted them to understand and appreciate, if not also to love. But the process only worked with rock and roll that was unusually verbal, and it never allowed any way of taking the music into account. Later, in the 1970s I taught popular detective stories along with *Oedipus Rex* and Harlequin romances along with the novels of Jane Austen, trying to find a way of linking high and low, and in those classes I began to notice the different ways in which I presented the material to students. "This is very easy," I would say about an assignment to read a supermarket romance. "You can knock this off in an hour or two." But then when we got to Jane Austen, I would caution my students to expect more. "This is one of the great novels of courtship. You will have to spend a great deal more time and care with this one, and besides, this one will really be on the final." My students, ever alert to what their teacher wanted, responded appropriately and read one as if it was easy and the other as if it was hard.

Eventually I changed my tactic, and by the 1980s I was asking students to buy the current newsstand edition of *Cosmopolitan* (ideal because it totally eliminated the possibility of students turning in old papers from fraternity or sorority paper files) and then to read it as if it were a tough and complex work of literature. But to do that we had to read Jane Austen first, in order to learn careful reading and then to understand the ways in which a great novelist used the problems of courtship as the basis for a novel. I therefore changed the order of the pairings, beginning with the great book and then moving on to the popular story. No longer was I leading my students from the easy to the difficult, but rather from the older to the more recent, and no longer was I making a distinction about quality or complexity or meaning. This is different from what other critics of popular culture have done. "There are romances as elaborate and arcane as Spenser's *Faerie Queene* and as simple as the comic strip adventures of Super-man and Batman," John Cawelti writes (*Six-Gun Mystique*, 70). But if you read *The Faerie Queene* first and then turn to Superman or Batman, you begin to see complexity in the popular form that you were unable to see before. Given my direction that *Cosmopolitan* was to be treated as a great work of literature, many of my students found complexity and paradox in it without much difficulty, and along with all that a great many parallels to Jane Austen (or Gustave Flaubert or Edith Wharton). *Cosmopolitan*, it turned out, is much closer to an Austen novel than to a Harlequin romance because it plays multiple stories off each other, sometimes quite seriously and at other times quite ironically, setting up contrasts that would do Austen proud. That taught me an important lesson, that how a story is presented to a reader determines at least in part how the reader will respond to it. It changed me as a teacher. I began treating a variety of popular texts as if they were great works of literature to see what would happen. This book is the result.

Most of my students have not been English majors, and although many of them have been extremely intelligent (and overworked), they come uneasily into literature classes that are required of them for graduation. The whole idea of literature or, worse yet, the great books, puts them off, but they love movies and television programs, and some of them have watched the same soap opera almost every day since they were in junior high school. I teach them some obscure classic such as John Webster's great Renaissance tragedy *The Duchess of Malfi*. They are not delighted, they have trouble with the poetry, they struggle to keep the names of the characters straight all the while that I am lecturing them on the finer points of the content. But then I turn on the television in the classroom and we watch ten minutes of *Days of Our Lives*. Half the class sits in rapt attention, suddenly comfortable, the other half much more dubiously, uneasy about the transition I am asking them to make. After we do ten minutes or so of soap-opera watching in every class meeting for a week or so, most of the other half of the class is also hooked. They want to keep watching! This is Jacobean revenge tragedy in modern dress, I tell my students at this point, and then I ask them to determine how much of what I have said about Webster remains true of *Days of Our Lives*. To challenges like this they have almost always responded enthusiastically, and many return to Webster with heightened interest.

Students who can remember what happened in *The Duchess of Malfi* only with the greatest of difficulty, usually under pain of failing the midterm, can lovingly recite the plot details of the last six months or six years of their favorite soap operas. When I point out how similar they are, the problem posed by my class changes and becomes one of discovering whether the playgoers of seventeenth-century England got a better revenge story than television viewers of the late twentieth century. A related question animates this book, since we cannot recover the experience of those earlier audiences: Who gets the better story, the people who watch the soap operas and the movies, or the people who read the great books in lit classes? This comparison between Jacobean revenge tragedy and contemporary soap opera is meant to be representative of the process, for I have done this with almost all of the paired sets of texts on which this book is based. I have taught *Star Trek* in classes devoted solely to popular culture, and *Gulliver's Travels* in classes devoted solely to satire or to the literature of the eighteenth century, but neither story as successfully as when I have joined them together in classes on popular culture and the great tradition. The simple direction to compare the stories animated one class for two weeks, producing a spirited argument as to which was the better story and what constituted good literature. The presence in the classroom of several students who were devoted *Star Trek* fans was essential to the unit's success. Literature demands respect and deference from students, but contemporary movies and television programs do not. In Walter Benjamin's terms, the great books have aura. In practical terms what this means is that students hesitate to be critical of *The Iliad* or *Gulliver's Travels* but feel more than capable of making sense of *Rambo* or *Star Trek*, and that is why the combination works well in a classroom.

This book has many purposes, one of which is to present a method of teaching literature. I no longer wish to lure my students from the story they love to the story I want them to understand and appreciate, if not also to love. Now I want them to understand the differences between the literature of the past, which is taught and preserved by the university, and the literature of the present, which surrounds them. Often they go away sobered by the differences, but sometimes they are charmed, and in either case I have given them a new way to understand television, movies, and other forms of popular storytelling, and a new tool to assist in that understanding, literary criticism, which no longer is useful only for making sense of the classics. The very same questions asked about a novel by Jane Austen or Gustave Flaubert can be asked of *Cosmopolitan*, and the same kinds of analysis made of the *Iliad* can be made of *Rambo*.

"Cultural power," Stuart Hall argues, depends on drawing "the line, always in each period in a different place, as to what is to be incorporated into 'the great tradition' and what is not. Educational and cultural institutions, along with the many positive things they do, also help to discipline and police this boundary" ("Notes," 236). English professors have tampered constantly with this boundary in the last twenty-five years, and as a result much new material has been incorporated into the curriculum. My concern here, however, is much broader, not with what is to be incorporated into the great tradition and what is not, but with the whole concept of the boundary. Following Hall, Andrew Ross writes that "cultural power does not inhere in the contents of categories of taste. On the contrary, it is exercised through the capacity to draw the line between and around categories of taste; it is the power to define where each relational category begins and ends, and the power to determine what it contains at any one time" (*No Respect*, 61). This is what my students have explored. The process itself is empowering because it is not only a study of line drawing, but an invitation to draw the line on one's own or to refuse to draw the line at all. Ross calls for "a thoroughgoing classroom critique of taste" that will "explode the 'objective' canons of aesthetic taste rather than simply reinforcing or expanding them by appropriating, as a new colony of legitimate attention, cultural terrain that was hitherto off-limits. . . . This means challenging the categorical function of canons rather than simply changing the nature of their contents" (212). This is what I have attempted to do here and what I have done in my classroom. Suggesting that *Rambo* and *The Iliad* are comparable works, I could hardly do otherwise.

"*Rambo* is just as good as *The Iliad*," I tell my students one day when we finish with both. "No, no," all of them reply, "*The Iliad* is many times better." "Well then," I say, "which would you rather spend time on, *Rambo* or *The Iliad*?" "*Rambo*," they reply in unison and without a moment's hesitation. For a while the room is silent while they face the meaning of their choice. But the problem of value judgment remains. On the one hand, there are arguments like those put forward by Pierre Bourdieu that "all cultural practices (museum visits, concert-going, reading, etc.), and preferences in literature, painting, and music, are closely linked to educational level . . . and secondarily to social origin" (*Distinction*, 1). We can trace this line all the way back to *The Elements of Criticism* in 1762, where Lord Kames wrote, "Those who depend for food on bodily labor are totally devoid of taste" (quoted in Wellek, *Attack*, 34). On the other hand, there are arguments such as those put forward by Neil Postman that "the decline of a print-based epistemology and the accompanying rise of a television-based epistemology has had grave consequences for public life, that we are getting sillier by the minute" (*Amusing Ourselves*, 24). These points of view are not easy to reconcile. Professors of literature are either imposing their own class-based and education-based

values on students or they are rescuing students from the sloth and
trivia that is engulfing them. My solution has been to ask students to
move back and forth between trash culture and the great books, and
to come to their own conclusions. The Greeks had *The Iliad* and the
tragedies of Euripides, whereas we have *Rambo* and *The National
Enquirer*. Did we get shortchanged? It is a question worth thinking
about carefully.

The Organization of the Book

The chapters that follow are arranged in order of increasing complexity. After a discussion of the critical context for understanding this
book (chapter 2), I present a section of case studies designed to make
the case as best I can that a wide variety of popular entertainment is
extremely similar to the great literature of the past: that *Star Wars*
replicates *The Faerie Queene* (chapter 3); that the trash TV talk show
is a synthesis of *Six Characters in Search of an Author* and *A Streetcar
Named Desire* (chapter 4); that sitcoms and soap operas like *Friends,
Seinfeld*, and *Days of Our Lives* are part of a much larger reworking
of the history of drama on commercial television (chapter 5); and that
supermarket tabloids and celebrity gossip magazines not only are very
similar to the great dramatic tragedy of the past, but they meet many
of the most important critical definitions of tragedy set up by scholars
and philosophers (chapter 6).

In the second section of the book I introduce the problem of value,
the problem that as contemporary storytellers rewrite the great tradition of literature they change what we are told should matter most
to us: that advertising takes up and subverts the tradition of utopia in
the interests of consumer society (chapter 7); that the shopping mall
similarly adapts the tradition of formal gardens to the needs of a consumer society (chapter 8); that *Playboy* is a *Book of the Courtier* for
an age of mechanical reproduction and rampant consumerism (chapter 9); and that *Cosmopolitan* reworks the tradition of the woman's
coming-of-age novel for new social and economic realities (chapter
10).

In the third section of the book I discuss the problem of politics and
history: that *Star Trek*, like *Gulliver's Travels* before it, is deeply involved in the politics and history of its own time and place (chapter
11); and, finally, that all of the major movies made about the war in

Vietnam from *Star Wars* in 1977 to *Born on the Fourth of July* in 1989 are reworkings of the great literature of the past, and that what passed for portrayals of Vietnam were really imaginative stories about what might have happened in other times and in other places (chapter 12). I conclude with a brief discussion of the issues presented in the book (chapter 13).

CHAPTER 2

The Critical Context

In a television advertisement for coffee, a well-dressed man arrives late for a small but elegant dinner party, too late for anything but the Taster's Choice instant coffee over which the other guests are lingering with pleasure. These are people for whom instant coffee is the fitting end to a festive meal. As luck would have it, he is seated next to the same attractive woman he has met in a previous advertisement for Taster's Choice coffee, which showed her knocking at his door to borrow some instant coffee for one of her elegant dinner parties. At that time they engaged in some flirtatious behavior over his jar of Taster's Choice, and now, preliminaries aside, he looks at her with suave sophistication, or insufferable smugness, and announces that he plans to invite her to his place for dinner. "How do you know I will accept?" she asks, eyes fluttering demurely. "You can't resist my coffee," he tells her, and the advertisement ends on this note, as she drinks deeply of the Taster's Choice coffee, although we know that there will be continued adventures in the years to come.

Such as it is, short and sexually suggestive, this drama would be familiar enough to the London theater audiences of the late seventeenth century for it is a very clever commercial replay of the most famous scene in all of Restoration comedy, the teapot episode from William Wycherley's *The Country Wife* where the rake-hero Horner and the married women he seduces, Lady Fidget and Mrs. Squeamish, talk to each other in terms of his teapot and the amount of tea he has left to offer the women who wish to admire its spout. Here Wycherley's moment of brilliant comic obscenity becomes crass commercial manipulation with the simple addition of product identification; had Wycherley only tried to sell his audience tea or teapots, instead of tickets to his play, his story would have been very close to what we see on American television. But this change also would have increased audience members' interactions with and awarenesses of the text because, armed with Horner's tea or his teapot, they might have been tempted to act out the fantasy they had seen on the stage or might simply have recalled the fantasy every time they drank the tea, becoming in the process much more involved with the story. Wycherley's drama would remain in their minds, or psyches, long after they had left the theater. Something changes in the nature of storytelling in the age of television, but something remains the same. The audience at Wycherley's theater paid admission at the door whereas the audience of the television commercial pays indirectly in terms of increased prices for goods and services and, perhaps more significantly, in terms of the stories themselves becoming commercial manipulations.

Is this good or bad? A generation ago Dwight Macdonald argued in a series of influential essays that mass culture was "a parody of High Culture" ("Masscult," 3), "fabricated by technicians hired by businessmen" (14). In his view, popular entertainment borrowed the forms of high culture, reduced their complexity, and then substituted infantile or worthless content. Macdonald would undoubtedly argue that the relationship between the Taster's Choice coffee ad and the teapot scene from *The Country Wife* perfectly illustrates such a destruction of art. But even though the advertisement is mass or popular culture, fabricated by technicians hired by businessmen, it is not a parody of Wycherley's play, only an imitation of something that is already a parody, and it is not any more infantile or less complex than the original scene. Certainly it is more commercial, just as *Cosmopolitan* is more commercial than *Madame Bovary* and rock and roll is more commercial than poetry. What is at issue here, however, is not the intrusion of modern economics into storytelling, but the extent to which something like this television advertisement is a trivialization of the great literature of the past. Why is the teapot scene from Wycherley any more or less profound than the coffee advertisement?

Many critics do argue, as Macdonald does, that popular entertainment trivializes high culture. Hans Magnus Enzenberger writes that "the dramaturgical clichés of mediocre screenplays: watered down beyond recognition . . . repeat traditional patterns taken from the drama and the novel of the past" (*Consciousness Industry*, 14), and Hannah Arendt maintains that "those who produce for the mass media ransack the entire range of past and present culture in the hope of finding suitable material" ("Society," 48). But the teapot scene from Wycherley is not watered down beyond recognition, nor are the other elements of great literature in contemporary trash culture. Arendt is right about the process of imitation, but her argument that writers of mass culture "ransack the classics" only reveals her deep-seated prejudice against popular forms of literature.

Since Kant's pronouncements on aesthetics two centuries ago we have been taught that art is something we experience from a detached point of view, something that has no immediately practical value for us, and on such grounds the Taster's Choice advertisement certainly cannot measure up to the teapot scene from the Wycherley play. Neither can something as pragmatic as *Cosmopolitan* hope to measure up to something as aesthetic as *Madame Bovary*. We do read Flaubert's novel quite differently than the magazine, of course: the first in university literature classes as an example of the triumph of naturalism in the nineteenth century, the second in everyday life as a practical guide to courtship in a society in which sex is one of the greatest powers granted to women. One is art, the other useful, or at least meant to be useful. But when Flaubert first attempted to publish *Madame Bovary* the French government was concerned that readers would take the novel as an endorsement of adultery, and it attempted to prevent the novel's publication. It wasn't art then, only pornography, and it is only now, many years later, that what once had very immediate meanings for its audience has settled quietly down into art so that we can approach it with the finer nuances of aesthetic detachment. Similarly, we approach *The Duchess of Malfi* quite differently than *Days of Our Lives*—the play as an example of post-Shakespearean drama, part of a long and complex history of the English theater, and the soap opera as a fascinating story about people we have come to care about deeply because we know so many intimate details about their personal lives, more than we know about most real people in our lives. One is art, distanced from us, which we process intellectually. The other is entertainment, and completely emotionally involving. When a story is new, and written for a time and place that still exists around it, the responses to it are often emotional and practical. Only later, as conditions change, does the story invite more detached responses. It begins as entertainment, didactic advice, or religious instruction and it ends as literature, in large measure because we are detached from it.

For most of the last two hundred years we have also been taught that art is special, as opposed to the ordinary, and that we are raised to a higher level of existence by great literature, something that we don't feel while watching television or going to the movies. Other definitions of art are even more grandiose: the "visible sign of an indwelling state of grace and harmony" (Mumford, *Art*, 23), "a massive blow from which one recovers slowly and which leaves one changed in ways that only gradually come to light" (Barzun, *Use*, 74). The transcendent specialness of art is a quality that we are willing to grant to a poet like Homer, but not to an actor like Sylvester Stallone. We also insist that art be consciously created as art. The editors of *The National Enquirer* are grinding out scandal-mongering gossip in order to sell newspapers in order to make money; Euripides, we feel, had finer motivations. All we do know is that he was a great storyteller, that his stories were performed at religious festivals where they were awarded prizes, and that they concerned the personal lives of larger-than-life religious figures and therefore had religious meanings. The contributors to *The National Enquirer* write shorter, less polished stories, which appeal to large numbers of people and which concern the personal lives of larger-than-life public figures and therefore have public meanings.

But if *The National Enquirer* would be dismissed by traditional aesthetic definitions, it may be art according to more recent critical formulations. Art is what the art world says is art, Arthur Danto (*Transfiguration of the Commonplace*) argues in what has become an influential point of view in contemporary aesthetics. When Marcel Duchamp puts a ceramic urinal on a block of wood and has it accepted for an exhibition, it becomes art at that moment. If a literary critic asserts that the *Enquirer* is literature, then it is literature. Matei Calinescu calls popular culture "the 'normal' art of our time," and writes, "we have to recognize that it is the obligatory starting point of any aesthetic experience" (*Faces of Modernity*, 258). If Calinescu is right, we need to treat this popular entertainment as carefully as we treat those other aesthetic forms, asking the same kinds of questions about it that we ask of art, without necessarily expecting the same kinds of answers. And because it does resemble those other forms of art, we can compare popular entertainment to great books in order to make its own meanings clear, a process that allows us to look at familiar materials in new ways.

Arnold, McLuhan, and Jameson

There is something in this book to offend almost everybody who works in the criticism industry. Traditional literary critics who are committed to Matthew Arnold's notion ("Culture and Anarchy") that we must nurture and preserve the very best that has been thought and said in culture will not appreciate my insistence on the fundamental similarity between great books and popular entertainment. No one who believes that Jane Austen, Gustave Flaubert, and Edith Wharton have created some of the greatest novels of the last two hundred years will be pleased by my argument that the editors of *Cosmopolitan* have replicated significant aspects of their work, albeit in flashy and commercial postmodern form, and that *Cosmo* should be considered a comparable accomplishment. Television and media critics who are committed to Marshall McLuhan's notion (*Understanding Media*) that each new medium is unique unto itself may be irritated by my insistence on the fundamental similarity between the content of great books and the content of television and media entertainment. No one who believes that the medium is the message will be pleased by my argument that the content of the medium is also the message, that *Days of Our Lives* is broadcasting contemporary versions of Jacobean revenge tragedy, or that *Rambo* can be considered the *Iliad* of the Vietnam War. Television critics have spent too much time and effort distancing themselves from literature and from literary critics in their successful efforts to build the discipline of television studies to be pleased to see an old position reasserted again. And contemporary cultural critics who are committed to Fredric Jameson's notion that we must always historicize will dismiss my insistence on the fundamental similarity between the great books of the past and the popular entertainment of the present. No one who believes that literary production is necessarily tied to the economic, social, and political conditions of its own time and place will be pleased by my argument that *Playboy* is very similar to Castiglione's *Book of the Courtier*. Too much must have happened in the history of sexuality for a popular American magazine to so thoroughly mimic a masterpiece from the Italian Renaissance. History should not allow this to happen.

I readily admit that *Cosmopolitan* is not the same kind of literature as a Jane Austen novel, but I would argue that it is the next stage of the traditional novel form, an illustrated collage of stories about the problems faced by a young woman in courtship that is just as suited to contemporary readers as the Jane Austen novel was for the readers of early-nineteenth-century England. *Days of Our Lives* is not the same kind of drama as *The Duchess of Malfi*, what with its incredible length, very slow pacing, and constant interruption by advertisements, but because its fundamental story lines so precisely replicate those in seventeenth-century English theatre, the medium is not the only message. Content also matters. And although attitudes toward sexuality may have undergone significant change between Castiglione and Hefner, *Playboy* is still extremely similar to *The Book of the Courtier*.

In his influential essay "Reification and Utopia in Mass Culture," Fredric Jameson argues that great works and popular entertainment are dialectical opposites of each other and thus appropriate for comparison, but only when these texts have been created in the same time period. For Jameson, it is pointless to compare Shakespeare and Charlie Chaplin. But although this may be true from a strictly historical point of view, it excludes a whole set of relationships between high culture and mass or popular culture that are also extremely important. The short stories about suffering and fall that fill the pages of *The National Enquirer* and its sister publications are fragments of tragedy, not as contemporary dramatists would write them, but as Euripides, Henrik Ibsen, and August Strindberg would. And although the stories in the *Enquirer* can be shown to be the dialectical opposites of Samuel Beckett's drama, that simply leads us back to the place where all inquiry about the relationship between high culture and popular culture begins, with the critical perception of difference. Jameson asks us to see that such texts are tied to each other as opposites, but I am interested in something else here, in continuity and similarity rather than opposition and difference. Although it may be very helpful to see that Beckett and the editors of the *Enquirer* are writing dialectically opposed stories of suffering and fall, what I hope to demonstrate here is that the editors of the *Enquirer* have taken over the tradition of tragedy from Euripides to Ibsen that had been abandoned by writers like

Beckett. This is the way of overcoming what Andreas Huyssen (*After the Great Divide*) has called "the great divide" between high and low, although we must be able to move freely through the history of literature in our search for the great books that contemporary trash culture replicates so carefully for us.

Popular writers certainly do. And if writers can cross the great divide irrespective of history, the critics who would understand their work must be able to do the same. We have, for example, already historicized *Rambo* as a movie of the 1980s, already situated it within the context of its own time, traced parallels with the Reagan presidency, the debate over American prisoners of war who might or might not still be alive in Vietnam, Reagan's subsequent understanding of himself as Rambo, and the conservative American political agenda of the 1980s. But although all of this is essential to any understanding of the movie, it is not all there is to say about *Rambo*. Cultural studies misses something extraordinary about the movie that we can only see when we approach it from the perspective of the great tradition of literature. Marx, Freud, and Foucault are not the only valuable sources for understanding a movie like *Rambo*; so too is Homer. And once we can recognize *Rambo* as our new version of *The Iliad*, then everything that we have already learned about the meaning of *The Iliad* can be applied to the political revision of history in front of us in order to understand how the movie works on us so powerfully.

Not everybody is happy about this. In his eloquent lament for *The Western Canon*, Yale critic Harold Bloom predicts that in the near future "what are now called 'Departments of English' will be renamed departments of 'Cultural Studies' where Batman comics, Mormon theme parks, television, movies, and rock will replace Chaucer, Shakespeare, Milton, Wordsworth, and Wallace Stevens" (485). But although Bloom would be appalled by my classroom, and even more by this book, his groundbreaking idea—that each great writer is responding to the specific challenges of a predecessor, whose work he or she rewrites—is the principle I apply here to popular storytelling. I don't know anything about Mormon theme parks, but I do know that the writers of *Rambo* take on *The Iliad* in the same way that Wallace Stevens takes on Walt Whitman, and that Rambo and *The Iliad* work extremely well together in a classroom. "Education founded upon *The Iliad*, the Bible, Plato, and Shakespeare remains, in some strained form, our ideal," Bloom writes, "though the relevance of these cultural monuments to life in our inner cities is inevitably rather remote" (31). What he does not realize, because he scorns the popular, is that contemporary versions of *The Iliad*, the Bible, Plato, and Shakespeare are pervasive in our culture. We do not get our *Iliad* untouched by history, but we do get it in a form that is emotionally meaningful for us and our children, in inner cities and suburbs and universities alike. I come not to bury Bloom's curriculum of great books, but to save it.

I mean this quite seriously. At a time when professors like Bloom complain bitterly about declining enrollments in the humanities and warn that English departments are about to go the way of classics departments (shrinking to near oblivion), large numbers of students make their way into my classes, not because they love the great books of the Western world but because they love movies and television programs. And because *Rambo* is contemporary America's *Iliad*, they are willing to look closely at Homer.

To accomplish this I must make connections between the old ways of telling stories and the new, and not everyone believes that this is either sensible or correct. "Not all forms of discourse can be converted from one medium to another," Neil Postman argues in *Amusing Ourselves to Death*. "It is naive to suppose that something that has been expressed in one form can be expressed in another without significantly changing its meaning, texture, or value" (117). Anyone who tries to read a new medium in terms of an old one, Postman tells us, is guilty, in Marshall McLuhan's terms, of "rear view mirrorism." McLuhan's phrase rests on one of the central principles of twentieth-century literary criticism, that any form of literature has to be judged by the criteria of its own form. Although McLuhan also asserts the opposite, that there is important continuity—"Any story line that television has is borrowed from other media" ("Television in a New Light," 90)—that argument has not proved as useful to media critics looking for ways to establish the independence and importance of their own discipline.

Following McLuhan, television critics John Fiske and John Hartley argue that any attempt to treat television as if it is literature is "not only doomed to failure but is also likely to result in a negative evaluation of the medium based on its inability to do a job for which it is in fact fundamentally unsuited." Television, they insist, is for the most part "subversive of the very values most prized by literacy" (*Reading Television*, 15). But are they right? Even if television is subversive of the values of literacy—note that neither Homer nor Euripides required any reading skills on the part of their audiences—television can still be evaluated against print literature, or dramatic literature, or oral literature with a little sensitivity and care. No one expects television to be precisely the same as the literature that has come before it, but its content, if not its form, is similar enough to allow intelligent connections to be made. To deny tradition and continuity is to isolate each new medium as a special case. We have learned how to compare epic poetry to drama and drama to the novel. Surely we can also compare the novel to movies and television. It is significant in this respect that in his more recent work Fiske has modified his earlier stand, admitting that "most popular television narratives conform more or less precisely" to the structure of Russian folk tales. "At times the conformity is astonishing in its precision" (*Television Culture*, 137).

It is not just partisans of television studies, like Fiske and Hartley, who have insisted on McLuhan's notion of the radical discontinuity between different media. Critics who denounce television with fear and loathing also assert this principle. Television, Alvin Kernan writes in *The Death of Literature*, "is not just a new way of doing old things but a radically different way of seeing and interpreting the world. Visual images not words, simple open meanings not complex and hidden, transience not permanence, episodes not structures, theater not truth" (151). Is he right? Perhaps. But television is also a new way of doing old things, and in this case television replicates literature, either consciously or—perhaps the more interesting possibility—accidentally. Visual images are different from words and communicate differently, but they do not have to be impoverished versions of words. W. J. T. Mitchell explains in *Iconology: Image, Text, Ideology* that "the history of culture is in part the story of a protracted struggle for dominance between pictorial and linguistic signs, each claiming for itself certain proprietary rights on a 'nature' to which only it has access" (43). A writer like Kernan presents his critique of popular culture in terms of that historical struggle. Thus Kernan argues that "literature's ability to coexist with television, which many take for granted, seems less likely when we consider that as readers turn into viewers, as the skill of reading diminishes, and as the world as seen through a television screen feels and looks more pictorial and immediate, belief in a word-based literature will inevitably diminish" (151). But there is another possibility to be considered, that television re-presents literature to us in more pictorial and immediate ways, something that has been hard to see because we are not used to studying television drama in the same ways that we study literature. Kernan explains that "the emphasis on the fine details of style that has characterized literature from the beginning is possible only with a stable printed text—imagine trying to follow a pattern of images, a series of linked ironies, a pattern of symbols in an oral performance!" (132). But with the videotape recorder that is exactly what we can do with television, and what we will find—not always, but often enough—is that stories that seem ordinary and commonplace turn out to be extremely interesting revisions and modifications of the great literature of the past. Once we can recognize that, we can also recognize them as extremely interesting works in themselves.

It is worth remembering that many of the men and women who write for television and the movies are literate, articulate, and highly educated, and some of them know the great tradition of literature as well as, if not better than, the English professors teaching in our colleges and universities. Grant Tinker, former production head of NBC, writes that the comedies of the eighteenth-century Irish playwright Richard Brinsley Sheridan gave him "a standard by which to judge literate comedy designed for a mass audience. Sheridan's style was very close to that of the best 'three-camera' comedies on television. . . . To me, he was a creative forerunner of . . . the world-class multiple-camera comedy writers. If Richard Brinsley Sheridan were alive today, he'd be winning Emmys" (*Tinker in Television*, 22). As the chapters to come should demonstrate, Tinker is not alone in using the great tradition, intelligently and effectively, to create contemporary entertainment.

The Continuity of Literature

There is a remarkable continuity between the great literature of the past and the popular entertainment of the present. Between Homer and *Rambo* many things remain the same about storytelling. Literary genres endure over time, adapted by different authors to different historical circumstances but with their essential natures relatively unchanged. Tragedy is not dead, as critics have claimed, it has simply appeared in places we have not looked to find it. The epic is not dead, nor has it degenerated into mere parody; it has simply changed from poetry to the movies. The two great forms of comedy devised in ancient Greece are still the two forms of comedy available to us today: the Old Comedy of Aristophanes now primarily in the movies, where it continues to celebrate the rebellious individual, and the New Comedy of Menander, Plautus, and their followers primarily on television, where it continues to celebrate domestic life.

Important differences between popular entertainment and great and enduring art do exist. The most obvious is the means by which they communicate: television and related forms of popular entertainment by images as well as by language, traditional literature exclusively by language. Literary language is often, but not always, elaborate, poetic, or at least very carefully chosen; the language of popular entertainment is often, but not always, ordinary and simple. Flaubert wrote *Madame Bovary* with a compulsion for finding just the right word; the editors of *Cosmopolitan* knock off an issue a month in the most ordinary language of daily life, relying on elaborate and provocative visual images in place of elaborate or elevated language. Flaubert spends pages describing a scene; in the magazine these scenes are communicated much more immediately by images. *The Iliad* is poetry; *Rambo* is made up of grunts, short cryptic dialogue, and other diminished uses of language. On the other hand, *The Iliad* is a construction made up entirely of words; *Rambo* has spectacular visual images and a flashy sound track. One is not necessarily better than the other, although most people prefer movies whereas most literary critics prefer the earlier form. Herbert Marcuse argues that the language of one-dimensional society "controls by reducing the linguistic forms and symbols of reflection, abstraction, development, contradiction; by substituting images for concepts" (*One Dimensional Man*, 103). But art historians and other lovers of images are not likely to agree. Etherege's comedy *The Man of Mode* is filled with balanced neoclassical language and sparkles with verbal wit; the television sitcom *Seinfeld* repeats the content of Etherege's play for the most part in the ordinary language of everyday life. For lovers of seventeenth-century language a great deal is lost, but there is a comparable gain in the close-ups of individual actors' faces and their subtle changes in expression, which would have been impossible for Etherege's theater to achieve. These differences are real, not to be denied, and they come from technology.

But deciding which is better, or which makes the better art form, is not so easy.

A second difference may seem to be the length and complexity of the work, but for every work of popular entertainment that is shorter or less developed than its comparable great book there is another that is longer and more developed. The *Enquirer* does not deal with a single story with the same care or detail as Euripides did, but it presents a great many of them jumbled together. *Rambo* is many times shorter than *The Iliad*, but the soap opera *Days of Our Lives* is much longer than the Jacobean revenge tragedy *The Duchess of Malfi*.

There are also differences in content, and these are potentially the most interesting differences because they suggest ways in which values have changed over time. With the exception of an obvious decline in religious faith, however, and a concomitant increase in consumerism, there are few consistent shifts from the great tradition to trash culture. When John Berger compared contemporary advertisements filled with things to the earlier history of oil paintings filled with things he concluded that "the oil painting showed what the owner was already enjoying" whereas advertising makes "the spectator marginally dissatisfied with his present way of life" (*Ways of Seeing*, 142). But there is a shift from dissatisfaction to satisfaction in the transition from *Gulliver's Travels* to *Star Trek*, and Berger's conclusion does not generalize. *Star Trek* is more positive than *Gulliver's Travels*, but *Good Morning Vietnam* is more negative than *The Acharnians*. *Cosmopolitan* is more optimistic than *Madame Bovary*, but *Rambo* is more pessimistic than *The Iliad*. Technology is celebrated in *Star Trek* but rejected in *Rambo*. No consistent pattern emerges, nothing that would allow for a clear and convincing thesis about dehumanization or decay. The complexities of literary history defy such simple, reductive answers.

The most important difference between trash culture and the great tradition, then, is the manner in which we experience them—intrusively in the case of entertainment, contemplatively in the case of the great tradition. Movies are loud, large, and frequently overwhelming; computer games require our active participation; television programs run almost constantly in many American homes. But a book is an object that you control, that you can close, put down, pick up again, and read at your own pace, that you can pull back from when you wish. Nothing like this is possible with the electronic media, and even in the popular print media, where glossy photographs of consumer goods and sexualized models can overwhelm the words, the psychological manipulations of the reader are powerful. This difference must not be minimized.

Similarly, we think of entertainment as escapist fun and great literature as tough and demanding food for thought and careful study. But the same care and attention can be paid to entertainment, and once it is, entertainment turns out to be almost exactly like the classics. An individual who reads, watches, or otherwise consumes popular entertainment, and an individual who reads, watches, or consumes great works of literature *would have comparable experiences*, providing that they asked the same sorts of questions and approached the material in the same sorts of ways. This book will ask those questions.

PART 1

Case Studies

A final possibility must be considered that printed literature, in the future, will be written for and read only by scholars. For the public at large it might give way to picture books, or to spoken and tape-recorded stories, or else to dramas and serials composed for television or the new medium that will come after that.

Whatever the new forms will be, I am not at all sure that I shall like them when they do appear. They won't be my forms and won't express my spirit, but I know they are needed if the new age is to become fully conscious of its own spirit.

Malcolm Cowley, *The Literary Situation* (1954)

CHAPTER 3

STAR WARS and
THE FAERIE QUEENE

A generation or so ago, some English professors will tell you, they could count on most of their students knowing the major books of the Old and New Testament, but the only story that virtually all of their students know today is *Star Wars*. They may shake their heads wistfully as they tell you this, and explain that there is no way to understand or appreciate the great English literature of the past without a solid background in the Bible. Something profoundly important has been lost to them as well as their students: a trilogy of science fiction action-adventure movies with extravagant special effects and clever marketing gimmicks has replaced the Bible as the primary story we share in common.

Because I am an English professor, I have heard my senior colleagues express their frustration and despair at this turn of events on more than one occasion, usually when we are arguing about the curriculum. I can report from personal experience that very few of my students have more than a vague idea about what is really in the Bible, even those who identify themselves as devout Christians, but virtually everyone knows and loves *Star Wars* (1977), *The Empire Strikes Back* (1980), and *The Return of the Jedi* (1983). When asked, many of my students will admit to having watched each of the movies well over twenty-five times, some more than one hundred times, while others explain that the assorted *Star Wars* action figures, light sabers, and spaceship models of their childhood are carefully packed away in their parents' basements, waiting for the time when their own children will play with them. Once I had a student who could recite the dialogue of one of the movies from memory, backwards or forwards; she was a very handy if somewhat unsettling resource to have in the classroom. Is this the way that previous generations of students knew the Bible? Perhaps. There are certainly some intriguing similarities.

I begin here with a consideration of *Star Wars* and its relationship to the great literature of the past because it has been so popular a story for us and because, for this current generation at least, it appears to have replaced the Bible as the urtext of our civilization. What does this mean for us? Nowhere is the contrast between contemporary entertainment and the great books of the past more extreme or significant. One of my colleagues once asked me how she could possibly teach her students a tough and demanding work of Renaissance literature like *The Faerie Queene* when all they knew or cared about were movies, television, and video games. Although I had no answer for her then, I do now, as least as regards *The Faerie Queene*, for from large themes to small details the *Star Wars* trilogy is a brilliant and meticulous cinematic retelling of *The Faerie Queene*. All of the major characters and plots of *Star Wars* are based on the major characters and plots of *The Faerie Queene*, which they repeat in ingenious and surprising ways. That means not only that a knowledge of *Star Wars* is an ideal starting point for any understanding and appreciation of *The Faerie Queene*, but also that a knowledge of *The Faerie Queene* is an ideal starting point for any understanding and appreciation of *Star Wars*. They are comparable stories and, I would argue, given the differences between the times of their composition, comparable achievements.

There are some obvious differences between them, the most important of which concerns language. What Edmund Spenser wrote in deliberately archaic poetic language for an audience of highly educated individuals at the end of the sixteenth century, Lucas has recast as a popular and accessible movie for an audience of American children and their parents toward the end of the twentieth century. In the process he has made a very large fortune, a fact I remind my students of when I describe the advantages of studying the classics. The age of print culture has given way to an age of show business, to borrow Neil Postman's term for it, an event that is not Lucas's fault, and although this does mean that our stories are less concerned with language and much more concerned with visual representation, it does not mean that they are any less interesting, brilliant, complex, or carefully crafted.

The Renaissance knew the process as *imitatio*, the adaptation of an important work or works of earlier writers, and it had a distinguished history before the age of copyrights, plagiarism, and intellectual property rights. Indeed, Spenser himself based much of *The Faerie Queene* on earlier epic poems, among them Ludovico Ariosto's *Orlando Furioso* and Torquato Tasso's *Jerusalem Delivered*, and because many of Spenser's readers knew Tasso and Ariosto, along with the Bible, they made the connections quickly enough. But because we perceive popular movies to have little in common with the great literature of the past, we would never connect a movie such as *Star Wars* to a poetic masterpiece such as *The Faerie Queene*. It would be too ridiculous. My colleague really did not expect me to come up with an answer to her dilemma about how to teach a great book with only the movies to refer back to; she just wanted to let me know how far we had fallen. But just as Spenser's poem was accessible to previous generations of readers because of their knowledge of the Bible, it is equally accessible to current generations of moviegoers because of their knowledge of *Star Wars*.

That is wonderful, for it means, among other things, that *The Faerie Queene* is known and loved by millions of people today, although in a radically different form from that revered by their book-loving English teachers. All of the doomsayers may be wrong about the sorry state of our cultural life after all, since it turns out that a cinematic adaptation of *The Faerie Queene* is the great urtext of our civilization. But whether Spenserians will rejoice over this news or not depends in large measure on what it is they love most about *The Faerie Queene*—the story Spenser tells or the way in which he tells it—since the special language of the poem is completely lost in the movies. I love the story. I know which version of the story my students prefer because I have often asked them: given a choice between the difficult vocabulary that often baffles them and makes them turn in frustration to *Cliffs Notes* and an exploding Death Star shown with a magnificent display of computer-generated special effects accompanied by thunderous noise and music, they'll take Lucas's Wagnerian adaptation any day over the Spenserian original. And who could blame them?

Is there a difference between studying *The Faerie Queene* in a college literature class because it will be on the midterm and watching *Star Wars* twenty-five times for the sheer pleasure of it? Of course. Is one better than the other? That is a more complex question, which involves the function of critical reading (and viewing), but it is important to remember that Spenser did not write his poem thinking it had a future as a subject on college examinations. He wanted to change his audience by delighting and instructing, and so did Lucas. "The generall end therefore of all the booke is to fashion a gentleman or noble person in vertuous and gentle discipline," Spenser wrote in his prefatory letter to *The Faerie Queene*. He tells us there that he selected historical fiction as his subject—now we might call it action-adventure—because it was the kind of story "men delight to read, rather for variety of matter, then for profite of the ensample" (*Faerie Queene*, 1). In an interview about his purposes in creating *Star Wars*, Lucas says: "I wanted to make a kid's film that would strengthen contemporary mythology and introduce a kind of basic morality" (Pollock, *Skywalking*, 144). The statements are extremely similar.

Spenser's poem is a long, elaborate, and imaginative sequence of stories, or books, about the knights of faerieland and their struggles to learn holiness, temperance, chastity, friendship, justice, and courtesy. In the first and most frequently taught book of *The Faerie Queene*, the part that serves as the basis for Lucas's story, the topic is holiness. The young and inexperienced Red Cross knight takes up the cause of an innocent woman named Una, fights an evil magician named Archimago, requires the help of a perfect knight named Arthur, learns religious faith from an old hermit named Contemplation, and finally masters holiness, an accomplishment that allows him to destroy the hellish monster that has taken control of Una's land. In Lucas's version of this story, the young and inexperienced Jedi knight Luke Skywalker takes up the cause of an innocent woman named Princess Leia, fights an evil magician named Darth Vader, requires the help of a less than perfect fighter named Han Solo, learns religious faith from two old hermits named Obi Wan Kenobi and Yoda, and finally masters the Force, an accomplishment that allows him to destroy the evil empire, the hellish monster that has taken control of Leia's republic. There are many stories about knights and evil magicians and monsters, and Lucas has acknowledged reading *The Hero with a Thousand Faces,* Joseph Campbell's analysis of the cultural monomyth about the adventures of a hero who ventures into a land of fantasy and danger.

But although Lucas does borrow some ideas from Campbell, along with specific incidents and imagery from *The Wizard of Oz* and *Snow White and the Seven Dwarfs*, it is Book One of *The Faerie Queene* that Lucas mines for most of his story.

Almost everything of importance that we see in the *Star Wars* movies has its origin in *The Faerie Queene*, from small details of weaponry and dress to large issues of chivalry and spirituality. A dazzlingly bright light shield represents the special force of Christian spirituality in *The Faerie Queene* just as a special-effects light saber represents a similar spiritual force in *Star Wars*. Both are instrumental in the battle against evil. A powerful lion protects Una and represents the natural world in Spenser, just as a lionlike humanoid named Chewbacca protects Luke and Leia and represents the natural world in Lucas. Una wears white and is accompanied by a dwarf, just as Leia wears white and is accompanied by two androids, C3PO and R2D2. And just as Una's dwarf gathers up weapons, gives directions and information when he can, and functions as a servant, C3PO and R2D2 do the same. There are numerous figures of darkness and night in Spenser, all dressed in black and associated with Hell; in Lucas, Darth Vader and the evil emperor are dressed in black and associated with the Death Star. Red Cross wears the image of a cross at the beginning of his story and Luke gains what appears to be a clerical collar near the end of his.

Both are counseled to trust a spiritual force in battle. Una tells Red Cross when he engages in his first victorious battle with the monster Error, "Add faith unto your force and be not faint" (Book I, canto i, stanza 18); Obi Wan tells Luke when he engages in his first victorious battle with the Death Star, "May the Force be with you." Shortly after slaying Error, Red Cross is covered in her vomit. Luke, caught on the Death Star early in his story, is trapped in a vast garbage compactor and must swim about in the muck. At the end of his story, Red Cross kills the horrible dragon who has captured Una's parents by shoving his sword into the monster's open mouth. At the end of the first *Star Wars* movie, Luke destroys the Death Star by flying his small plane toward the planet's tiny hole and dropping in his bomb. Red Cross's victory is tempered by the escape of the archvillain Archimago, Luke's victory by the escape of the archvillain Darth Vader. Arthur cuts off the left arm of the giant Orgoglio in the middle of Spenser's story, and at the end Red Cross cuts off a paw of the dragon who has imprisoned

Una's parents. A short time later the dragon dies. Darth Vader cuts off Luke's hand in the middle of Lucas's story, and at the end Luke cuts off Vader's. A short time later Vader dies.

The major thematic preoccupations of *Star Wars* are the major thematic preoccupations of *The Faerie Queene*. The House of Pride in Spenser, filled with a variety of evil creatures with names like Idleness, Gluttony, Wrath, and Avarice, becomes the Saloon of Pride in Lucas, filled with a variety of evil creatures, one of whom is wrathful and another named Greedo. These are both glittery, seductive, and dangerous places. Red Cross is attacked by the evil knight Sansjoy in the House of Pride, Luke by an ugly and wrathful humanoid in the Saloon of Pride. A female version of the devil named Lucifera rules over Spenser's House of Pride; the devil himself is briefly but clearly shown in Lucas's saloon. In Spenser there is also a House of Holiness where Red Cross receives his spiritual training from a series of characters with names like Faith, Hope, Charity, and Contemplation, just as there is a place of holiness in Lucas, a jungle somewhere in the Degova system where Luke receives his spiritual training from Yoda. Faith shows Red Cross the power of Christianity by moving the sun, parting flood waters, and transporting mountains; Yoda shows Luke the power of the Force by raising up his smashed airplane.

There is also an important episode of sexual temptation and fall in Spenser when Red Cross embraces Duessa and "pourd out in loosnesse on the grassy grownd" (I, vii, 7), following which the "hideous" giant Orgoglio appears and imprisons Red Cross in his dungeon. Although it is much more muted, there is a similar episode in Lucas, when Luke physically approaches Leia when she is dressed in her sexy woman outfit, following which the hideous giant Jabba the Hutt imprisons Luke in his dungeon. In Spenser there is an episode with forest-dwelling satyrs, primitive creatures who rescue Una when her life is in danger, and in Lucas an episode with forest-dwelling Ewoks, primitive creatures who rescue Luke, Leia, Han Solo, and the droids when their lives are in danger. The satyrs worship Una as their god; the Ewoks worship the android C3PO as a god. *Star Wars* really is *The Faerie Queene* in modern dress.

Lucas does change Spenser's story, as some of these examples begin to suggest, adapting the Elizabethan poem to contemporary American realities. The desirable religion in *The Faerie Queene* is Protestant Christianity, caught up in battle with a depraved Roman Catholicism—Spenser was a partisan in the religious struggles of his time; the desirable religion in *Star Wars* is the nonsectarian Force, a generalized inner spirituality that echoes Eastern mysticism. Arthur is the perfect British knight in *The Faerie Queene*, a symbol of the might that will be England, straight, sober, and good; Han Solo is a flawed and fallen fighter who must be redeemed in *Star Wars*, a symbol of a peculiarly American wisecracking daredevil. In *The Faerie Queene* the spiritual and passive Una is contrasted with her opposite, the sensual and active Duessa, whereas Leia takes on both roles in *Star Wars*, appearing most often in white but once in a sexy outfit while she is chained to the revoltingly slimy monster, Jabba the Hutt. Women are much more complex in Lucas's version of the story.

Virtually every change Lucas makes in Spenser's story has the effect of increasing complexity. What works perfectly in *The Faerie Queene*, or at least is presented without ambiguity, is now harder, mixed, and much more difficult. At the end of his spiritual training and in the presence of Contemplation, Red Cross sees a vision of the city of god in the clouds and is overjoyed, for this is the New Jerusalem of Christian revelation. It is a sign that he is saved, that he has mastered the Force and is ready to fight the dragon. Lucas makes this more dramatically interesting for contemporary audiences by altering some crucial details. In the middle of his spiritual training and in the presence of Yoda and Obi Wan Kenobi, Luke sees a vision of his friends in a city in the clouds and is afraid, for it is the fortress of Lando Calrissian, where they are about to be taken prisoner by Darth Vader. He wants to go off and save them in spite of Yoda's warnings that he has not yet mastered the Force. The change is similar to Lucas's substitution of Han Solo for Arthur and the Ewoks for the satyrs. Good is less powerful in *Star Wars*.

But perhaps the greatest change in the story involves the shift in focus from the problems of sex and religion to the problems of power and politics. Duessa, who stands for the evils of the sensual Roman Catholic Church, tempts Red Cross to fall sexually and thus also spiritually, and his lack of physical control in her presence is his greatest vulnerability. Luke's father, Darth Vader, who stands for the evils of American imperial militarism, tempts him to fall by urging him to join the dark side of the Force so that they can rule the universe together, and Luke's lack of emotional control in the presence of his father is his greatest emotional weakness. By shifting the focus of the story in this way from a young man's relationship with a woman who has given in to the dark side of passion and love, to a young man's relationship with a father who has given in to the dark side of power, not only does Lucas make the story more appropriate for his target audience, children, but he also turns Spenser's poem about the evils of the other side's religion into a commentary on the evils of our own side's war in Vietnam, the immediate political context in which these movies were created. Luke's struggle with his father, who has gone over to the side of the militaristic empire, reflects the experience of many draft-age young men who struggled with their pro-war fathers over the morality of that war. Our temptation as a country was world domination, not sexual excess.

I will return to a consideration of the political context of the *Star Wars* movies later in this book, where I will contrast it with other movies about the war in Vietnam. What I wish to establish here is that although Lucas alters Spenser's story for new political realities, he does not change the fundamental structure of the story, for just as Red Cross is torn between Una and Duessa, representations of good and bad religion as well as pure and corrupt lovers, Luke is torn between Obi Wan Kenobi and Darth Vader, representations of good and bad social systems as well as pure and corrupt fathers. It is not a pure adaptation of *The Faerie Queene*, then, that we get with *Star Wars*, but a thoughtful and meaningful revision with a clear shift in focus. Strong poets revise and correct the work of other strong poets, Harold Bloom argues, and although he would reject the comparison I am making here between a great Elizabethan poet and a popular contemporary moviemaker, I would argue that George Lucas is a strong creator revising and correcting the work of a predecessor poet. The fact that *Star Wars* is aimed primarily at children does not reduce its significance or complexity for, as my students have remarked to me many times when our comparisons of Spenser and Lucas have required us to look carefully at *Star Wars*, almost none of the meanings of the movie are obvious to the children in the audience. *Star Wars*, like *The Faerie Queene*, can be appreciated as pure action-adventure. The real fun comes later.

English teachers typically dismiss movies that large numbers of people love as gross oversimplifications of complex issues, while elevating the poems, plays, and novels that they have devoted their lives to studying as sustained and complex explorations of the meanings of human existence. This contrast is not true for *Star Wars* and *The Faerie Queene*. Lucas's work is not a comic-book version of *The Faerie Queene*, but a substantial and complex adaptation of a literary classic that is a major achievement in its own right.

There are a number of reasons why *The Faerie Queene* is a great book, criteria we might use to evaluate *Star Wars* as well. What is most extraordinary about Spenser's poem from a reader's point of view is the extent to which the author is able to sustain the story, incident after incident, adventure after adventure, tailoring each book to a different knightly quality; the extent to which he is able to write in incredibly dense and inventive language, to say nothing of sustaining the rhyme scheme; the extent to which he is able to construct all of this as allegory, with characters representing such qualities as Protestantism and Catholicism, Law and Lawlessness; and the extent to which he is able to include in all of this a constant stream of allusions to the Bible, Tasso, Ariosto, Dante, Virgil, Homer, and classical mythology. The poem is a virtuoso display of his skill as a poet and his knowledge of religion, literature, and history. And in all this Spenser has distinct advantages over Lucas, for although *Star Wars* also functions as allegory—Lucas has explained that he modeled the evil emperor on Richard Nixon, and Yoda as an Asian wise man bears certain obvious resemblances to Ho Chi Minh—there are limitations to what he can expect of his audience of children. Spenser can echo *The Book of Revelation*, *The Odyssey*, and *The Divine Comedy*, counting on his educated adult readers to know the references, but Lucas can echo only *The Wizard of Oz* and *Snow White and the Seven Dwarfs*. This should not be taken as a sign that we have fallen from grace since the Renaissance, only that our children know different stories than sixteenth-century adults did.

The epic of the age of show business is not exactly like the epic of the age of print culture, but we have known that from the start. Does the child who watches the *Star Wars* movies get a story that is equal to *The Faerie Queene*? Absolutely. Would Spenser have enjoyed watching the *Star Wars* movies? Without a doubt, he would have loved them, especially since Lucas only does to him what he had done in his turn to the epic writers before him. George Lucas is the greatest Spenserian of our time.

CHAPTER 4

The Trash Talk Show

At the same time that English professors have been despairing about the stories their students know, numerous other critics have been despairing about what the rest of us have been watching on TV. And although there is much to choose from, the trashiest, most vulgar programs on television today may be the down-and-dirty, tell-all, confessional talk shows that turn the passions, ethical failings, and psychological traumas of ordinary men and women into popular entertainment. Every day an embarrassing parade of semiliterate human beings glories in their fifteen minutes of humiliation and suffering on what can only be described as a cross between soap opera and *The Gong Show*. According to the educators, politicians, and moralists who have pressured broadcasters to take these programs off the air, this is television at its very worst, a celebration of abnormal behavior that is an affront to American values and a danger to our impressionable children. And yet, for all of its obvious excesses, the trash talk show is also extremely similar to two of the most critically esteemed plays of the modern theater, Luigi Pirandello's *Six Characters in Search of an Author* and Tennessee Williams's *Streetcar Named Desire*. A synthesis of these plays, the trash talk show is the next logical development in the history of the theater and an exciting new form of improvisational drama.

What Ricki, Montel, Geraldo, Jerry, and their various followers are doing on television today is almost exactly what Luigi and Tennessee did on the stage before them. To be sure, they are doing it now with real people rather than dramatic characters, but such a situation is itself the main subject of *Six Characters in Search of an Author*, in which "real" characters struggle to tell their story to the audience without benefit of author or actors. In its dramatic format, which dispenses with the traditional structure of a well-made play, the talk show is like *Six Characters in Search of an Author*. In its most typical content, the dynamics of a large dysfunctional family or the sexual behavior of a misfit or predator, the talk show is like *Six Characters in Search of an Author* and *A Streetcar Named Desire*. In the theater we see misfits, predators, and wounded children as dramatic characters and praise them as the special creations of genius, but on our television sets we see them as real people and damn them as repulsive creeps. We have different standards for art and for life.

Is it this that makes Ricki and Geraldo and Jerry seem so bad and Luigi and Tennessee so good? After all, the talk-show hosts do let real people go at each other, not fully understanding what might happen, in a kind of theatrical free-for-all, whereas the playwrights script it all out carefully for their actors and directors. This surely is an important difference, although Pirandello's play says, quite explicitly, that this kind of theatrical scripting is phony and cannot possibly approach the truth of real characters who have real stories to tell. *Six Characters in Search of an Author* is a call for a less structured but much more honest kind of theater, without authors or actors, where characters are free to tell their own stories as best they can. For this groundbreaking work Pirandello was hailed as a genius and awarded the Nobel Prize for literature. This is also what the producers and directors of confrontational talk shows have achieved by pandering to the most vulgar interests of a television audience that has responded extremely positively to this kind of impromptu dramatic performance. What Pirandello predicted would be necessary has come into being not as a creation of a brilliant group of avant-garde playwrights, but because of the demands of the commercial marketplace.

There are real dangers in this attempt at television vérité, of course, since the human beings who appear as guests on the talk shows can and sometimes do hurt each other when the taping is over. In a celebrated incident in 1995, one man killed another after both had been guests on *The Jenny Jones Show*. *Six Characters in Search of an Author* ends with a fatal shooting on the stage, and although none of the surviving characters can tell for sure whether it is real or part of the play, this is only clever theatrical playing with appearance and reality in Pirandello. What the avant-garde theater of Pirandello could only pretend to do, the confessional talk show does for real. It is no wonder, then, that this kind of TV draws so many viewers: a new form of gritty improvisational theater is being born in front of us. Although it certainly turns human suffering into entertainment, so have all the great forms of drama that have come before it.

Like the characters in Pirandello's play who gather together on a stage, driven to tell the story of their dysfunctional family in spite of the fact that no "author" is available to shape their experiences into a play, the guests on the confessional talk show gather on such a stage and tell such stories about their lives, haltingly, imperfectly, and incompletely, while a host makes sure that they don't forget the most lurid melodramatic details. The characters in the Pirandello play do not agree on the relevant facts and squabble incessantly with each other about exactly what happened. So do the guests on the confrontational talk show. In Pirandello's play, six characters appear in a theater where actors and a director are rehearsing a play and announce that they are seeking an author to turn the raw material of their lives into drama. The father asks the director to take the role, but when he sets about arranging for his actors to learn from these characters, the characters make it clear that they wish to hold the stage themselves. And although the director is incredulous, the characters are real and believable, as Pirandello goes on to show, but the actors are not. Bound by the conventions of the stage, these actors are unable to capture any of the truth of the characters' story, producing only sentimentalized clichés.

Gradually we learn the details of the characters' squalid lives: that many years earlier the father grew bored with the mother and arranged for her to take up with a lover, that she had three children with this lover, and that now one of these illegitimate children, the stepdaughter, works in a house of prostitution where the father has been a regular customer. Here one of the crisis points of the play takes place. Although the father engages the services of the stepdaughter and asks her to undress, it is unclear whether any sexual intimacy takes place. The characters argue about whether the father recognizes the stepdaughter in time, but the mother, who insists that she has interrupted them, is particularly traumatized. Another crisis point occurs at the end of the play when the youngest child is discovered drowned in a fountain and another son shoots himself. Does this son hold himself responsible for the drowning, and is he in fact responsible, or is the shooting related to his own place in the troubled family? Whatever connection there might be between these events and the earlier sexual crisis in the family—which would be made clear in a well-made play—is lost in the chaos on the stage as the actors and manager rush about, unsure whether the boy is really dead or whether the whole thing has been an elaborate bit of playacting. The play ends without resolution, although we know that there is much more about the family than we have been told.

The families that appear on the talk show are often just like this. On one program, typical of the form, a stressed-out mother is introduced on the stage along with her twin sixteen-year-old daughters and their disapproving and controlling stepfather. They start squabbling almost immediately as they try to answer the host's simple questions. The daughters have run away from home many times since they were fourteen, when the mother married the stepfather. One of the daughters has just had a baby out of wedlock and now has a new twenty-seven-year-old boyfriend. She wants custody of her baby, but the mother and stepfather claim that she is unfit and want custody themselves. The host points out that the mother has not been able to care for the daughter, and the mother points out that her daughter does not know who the father is. The stepfather speaks contemptuously of the daughter, and both daughters blame the stepfather for everything that is wrong in their lives. More family members appear on the stage, including the stepfather's younger brother and his wife, both of whom take the side of the daughters. A sixteen-year-old boyfriend of the other daughter curses the mother and the stepfather. The mother's twelve-year-old daughter tells her sisters that she does not want them to return home. The grandmother denounces the mother and the stepfather. It goes on for an hour like this in a theatrical spectacle straight out of Pirandello, although it costs a great deal less to produce. Instead of paid actors, the talk show has found a gold mine of volunteers.

But if the talk show repeats Pirandello when the subject is families, when the subject is couples, the talk show more frequently takes its inspiration from Tennessee Williams, in particular the tangled sexual dynamic acted out by Stanley Kowalski, his wife Stella, and her sister Blanche Dubois in *A Streetcar Named Desire*. This is the talk show's great subject, the unrepentant male stud surrounded by the women with whom he has had sex, without regard for the consequences. In Williams's play Stanley beats his wife and rapes his sister-in-law, while Stella puts up with the abuse because she does not want to lose the great sex and Blanche—herself a sexual rule-breaker with a preference for underage boys—thinks she can control Stanley by flirting with him. Some variant of this conflict plays over and over again on the talk-show circuit, where two sisters or three cousins or four best friends or five girls in the neighborhood learn that they have been sleeping with the same man, who has betrayed them all. The women and the man sit very tensely on chairs, weeping or smirking and sometimes striking each other, as the TV host feigns shock and asks questions. "Did you know that your fiancé made love to your cousin on your living room floor?" "No, I did not," a stunned woman admits, while her cousin sits nearby gloating. "I can't help it if you can't keep your man," she says, and the first woman jumps out of her chair and moves to hit her cousin, stopped at the last minute by male stagehands. The studio audience goes crazy and the host grins while the guilty male stares dumbly at the floor between the various women with whom he has slept.

Blanche, Stella, and Stanley have abandoned the theater for the talk-show circuit, and although they no longer have a complete play to act out, with a beginning, a middle, and an end, the audience seems only interested in the juicy parts of their story anyway, in the moments of confession, recognition, and mayhem. We get the basic elements of Williams's drama without any of his theatrical refinements, without his stress on language, symbolism, and larger thematic meanings. But if there is nothing fancy here, this raw core is what makes Williams's best drama so powerful, the overwhelming sexual conflict in the lives of characters torn between their passions and traditional concepts of morality. This is the dynamic the trash talk show exploits so effectively. As a series of deeply troubled guests tell their stories about out-of-control sexual drives and members of the studio audience stand up to denounce abnormal behavior, American trash television pays homage to Tennessee Williams.

But there is one small if significant difference. At the end of the play, as Blanche is about to be incarcerated in a mental hospital because Stella will not believe that Stanley raped her, it is obvious that she has been completely destroyed. "I couldn't believe her story and go on living with Stanley," Stella tells a neighbor who likely knows the truth. "Don't ever believe it," the neighbor replies. "Life has to go on. No matter what happens, you've got to keep on going." Because Stella and Blanche are rivals for the attention of a man and therefore do not trust each other, Stanley wins in the end. But on the trash talk show, where the male stud is typically exposed by the host, who wants the women to understand how they have become his victims, this is not at all how it works. Like an indignant member of the audience of *A Streetcar Named Desire*, the host wants these women to do better than Stella and Blanche; they are, after all, real people. The male stud may not change, but at least the women leave the program with greater awareness, and that cheers the audience as the credits roll.

CHAPTER 5

FRIENDS, SEINFELD, and
DAYS OF OUR LIVES

To understand that the trash talk show is a contemporary variation on Luigi Pirandello's *Six Characters in Search of an Author* and Tennessee Williams's *Streetcar Named Desire* is to catch a glimpse of something much more remarkable, that variations on many of the great plays of the past appear on television today in new commercial formats, so many, in fact, that anyone who watches sitcoms and soap operas on a regular basis will see a good part of classic theatrical repertoire. *Friends* replicates most of the plots, character types, and themes of Shakespeare's melodramatic comedy *Much Ado about Nothing; Seinfeld* nearly all of the plots, character types, and themes of George Etherege's Restoration comedy of manners *The Man of Mode*; and episodes of *Days of Our Lives* all of the complex patterns of intrigue and deception of John Webster's Jacobean revenge tragedies *The White Devil* and *The Duchess of Malfi*. Beyond these examples, with which I will be concerned here, *Cheers* is very similar to Richard Brinsley Sheridan's *School for Scandal*, and *The Simpsons* to Oliver Goldsmith's *She Stoops to Conquer*. An episode of *Murphy Brown* repeats Molière's *Imaginary Invalid*, episodes of *A Different World* repeat Ben Jonson's *Volpone*, and episodes of *Knots' Landing* repeat William Congreve's *Way of the World*.

Commercial television is not so much a vast wasteland, as some of its critics have charged, but a magnificent postmodern warehouse overflowing with some of the great drama of the past. And although

these plays are re-presented to us in a jumble of adaptations that ignore the historical contexts of the originals, we do get to see a good
part of the history of theater on our TV sets without ever being aware
of it. And what we don't see on television we can watch at the movies,
where Francis Ford Coppola's *Godfather* trilogy is a contemporary
retelling of Aeschylus's *Oresteia* trilogy, Rodney Dangerfield's *Back
to School* repeats much of Aristophanes' *Clouds*, and Oliver Stone's
Platoon echoes Shakespeare's *Henry the Fourth, Part I*. In one form
or another, many of the masterworks of Western drama from Aeschylus to Tennessee Williams are readily available to us today as popular entertainment: we can see more of the great plays of the past,
more often, and more easily, than anyone who ever lived between the
ages of Aeschylus and Tennessee Williams.

But for anyone who loves the great theater of the past this is a mixed
blessing at best, since we do not get to see perfectly rendered copies
of the originals. Theater does change, especially on television, where
everything is packaged into thirty-minute or sixty-minute episodes and
constantly interrupted with commercials about the joys and sorrows
of domestic life. *Friends* may have taken Shakespearean comedy out
of the high-culture environment of the live stage and turned it into
must-see TV for a generation of young viewers, eliminating in the
process the poetic language of Shakespearean drama. If that seems a
horrible falling off from the standards of the past, especially to lovers
of Elizabethan poetry, it is worth remembering that Shakespeare communicated in words and television communicates by way of images.
We have learned to read the meaning behind the subtle raising of an
eyebrow or the slight twist of a head, nuances that would have been
impossible in the Elizabethan theater. Similarly, *Seinfeld* has taken
Restoration comedy out of the college drama anthologies and made
it vital and meaningful again to large numbers of enthusiastic viewers
who have never even heard of George Etherege and could not care
less, but it is also a gentler version of *The Man of Mode,* with little of
the cruelty or tough-minded characterizations of the original. Women
are much stronger and men much weaker in the sitcom, and if that
seems a great loss for lovers of authentic Restoration comedy, where
seductive men are usually gloriously successful, the world has changed
since the late seventeenth century and it is only reasonable that the
drama should reflect it. *Days of Our Lives* has brought the substance
of John Webster's great Jacobean revenge tragedies to soap-opera

audiences, but not without radically changing the form of the story. Webster's dramas last for less than three hours on the stage and then end with absolute finality; *Days of Our Lives* takes more than three months of programs at five hours each week to present comparable stories, and even then nothing is really over for good. This may seem extremely silly to viewers accustomed to the conventions of the traditional theater, but soap opera uses its extended playing time to great advantage, setting up extensive patterns of repetition in its various story lines that invite its viewers to make moral discriminations between very similar actions and events. There are important trade-offs in the wholesale appropriation of, or brilliant reinterpretation of, our theatrical heritage by the entertainment industry, but no sellouts.

Friends

Friends is *Much Ado about Nothing* transplanted to a New York City coffee shop, with Ross and Rachel as the inexperienced lovers Hero and Claudio, Chandler as the witty Benedict, Monica as the outspoken Beatrice, Joey as the worldly Don Pedro, and Phoebe as a generic Shakespearean fool. In the TV sitcom, as in the Shakespearean comedy, a small group of unmarried young men and women flirt with each other, play a series of tricks on each other, and fall in and out of love. Some of them are apprehensive and fearful about marriage and commitment, others much more enthusiastic, but all are torn between the conflicting obligations of love and friendship. A wedding ends in disaster when one person abandons the other at the altar. A man keeps women at a distance by his compulsive joking. A man and woman become lovers only when they learn by accident how much each loves the other. A woman who has been badly hurt by the man she loves requires that he suffer abject humiliation before she will accept him again. A young couple is torn apart by jealousy. A woman who is quiet and conventional slowly begins to gain confidence and, with it, her voice.

Ross loves Rachel in the first few seasons on the sitcom just as Claudio loves Hero in the Shakespearean comedy. The men are incredibly shy, unsure of themselves because of their inexperience with love and sexuality, and more than a little stiff. The women are young and beautiful, still in the process of finding themselves, but strong in their own ways. They are contrasted with their opposites: Ross with the sexually active, goofy Joey, who is always successful with women, and with the witty Chandler, who never is (at least in the early seasons of the program); Claudio with the sexually active and witty Benedict and with Don Pedro, a man who knows exactly how to woo women and is more than willing to help his friends. Rachel is similarly contrasted with the outspoken, off-beat Phoebe and with the independent Monica, just as Hero is contrasted with the outspoken, independent Beatrice. Four friends in Shakespeare become six on prime time, but the dynamics between them remain extremely similar. Chandler is the sitcom's version of Benedict, the witty, sarcastic bachelor who keeps himself from getting attached to women by thinking about their faults. But whereas Benedict meets his match in Beatrice, Shakespeare's strong and witty woman who trades jibes with him and ultimately marries him, Chandler does not find such a partner, as least not in the first years of the sitcom's run on television. That part of Shakespeare's story remains incomplete. And through it all, Phoebe wanders like a typical Shakespearean fool, making off-the-wall comments and singing songs that contain more than their share of truth.

Beyond character and plot, the creators of *Friends* generate meaning in much the same way Shakespeare did, by setting up dramatic contrasts between innocent and experienced lovers, clowns and scoundrels, good tricks and bad, agony and elation, and, perhaps most important, comedy and melodrama. The sitcom, like the Shakespearean comedy before it, moves abruptly between scenes of comic fun and foolishness and scenes of melodramatic pain and suffering. The pain is somewhat different, however, for although there is an active source of villainy in Shakespeare's comedy, the evil Don John, the melodramatic characters in the sitcom (such as Chandler's psychopathic roommate) are not part of the permanent cast and are exposed before they can do any real harm. The melodramatic moments on *Friends* come from honest misunderstandings rather than from manipulative villains.

In situation, character, plot, and structure, then, *Friends* is extremely similar to *Much Ado about Nothing*, and it leads to similar thematic preoccupations. What does love require of us? *Much Ado about Nothing* asks, and *Friends* most certainly asks the same thing in the same ways. Claudio and Ross are too naive and sentimental, Benedict and Chandler too scared and demanding, Hero and Rachel too young and insecure. They stumble around, along with the rest of their friends, until they can learn more about themselves and the nature of love and, in the process, become more lovable. Beatrice asks Benedict to reject his friends who have treated Hero so badly, and he does, although not without the greatest difficulty. Rachel asks Ross to accept her for who she is, faults and all. And all of them gain self-knowledge, lose isolation, and prove themselves in a test or difficult task. The comic view of life wins out over the anticomic view of life. Love and sex overcome evil and hate. The evil Don John, who tries to keep the lovers apart, fails when the clown Dogberry discovers the truth of his plot and lets the others know. Joey gets a job acting on the soap opera *Days of Our Lives*, but the anticomic melodrama seems merely ludicrous, false, and inconsequential in the context of the sitcom.

But not every element of Shakespeare's story form survives unchanged in the sitcom. At the beginning of *Much Ado about Nothing* Claudio wants to get married and doesn't understand anything about it, and Benedict understands marriage and doesn't want any part of it. They change, and the play ends with the double marriages of Beatrice and Benedict, and Hero and Claudio. In the very first episode of *Friends* Rachel leaves her fiancé Barry at the altar, and Ross's wife Carol leaves him when she discovers she is a lesbian. Nobody thinks marriage is a particularly good idea at this point in the story, and although Ross and Rachel become lovers later in the story line, they do not marry. There is a different attitude toward marriage here—which we can assume reflects our own time's attitude toward marriage, which is different from that of Shakespeare's time. The lovers in *Friends* still win out over the blocking forces that would keep them apart and still celebrate their erotic victory, but just as soon as they do, a new story starts up, which requires them to start the process all over again in what is essentially a new take on the comedy. It is worth remembering, however, that not everybody gets married in *Much Ado about Nothing*, and some critics argue that the play is a tough-minded consideration of whether marriage is the best arrangement for human happiness. And so is *Friends*.

Because the television program can go for years if it is successful whereas the Shakespearean comedy ends in a few hours, Ross and Rachel can replay the various complications of the courtship of Hero and Claudio almost indefinitely. In later episodes, for example, the lovers separate again, jealous, possessive, and confused once more,

and we are back to the situation faced by Hero and Claudio before
their humiliation, self-knowledge, and growth. Is this change simply
silly, undramatic, and predictable? The story of courtship as enacted
by *Friends* is actually far closer to the contemporary audience's experiences of love than the beginning-middle-and-end drama composed
by Shakespeare. Drawing the Shakespearean comedy out into years
of episodes changes but does not destroy the power of the story. It
may, in fact, enhance it.

Seinfeld

Seinfeld is *The Man of Mode* as it could be acted out only by a group
of deeply neurotic New Yorkers, with Jerry Seinfeld, George Costanza, Cosmo Kramer, and Elaine Bennes playing the parts of the
seductive rake Dorimant, his best friend Medley, their comically inappropriate foil Sir Fopling Flutter, and the woman who is the rake's
equal, Harriet Woodville. The parallels here are precise and extensive.
Seinfeld is a stand-up comedian and a fastidious dresser who seduces
and then loses interest in a series of women, just as Dorimant, who is
a great wit and a fastidious dresser, seduces and then loses interest in
a series of women. George Costanza follows Jerry around just as Medley follows Dorimant. Seinfeld's opposite is his comically outrageous
neighbor, Cosmo Kramer, a man with preposterously grandiose conceptions of himself who dresses in the style of a previous age; Dorimant's opposite is the pretentious fop Sir Fopling Flutter, a man with
preposterously grandiose conceptions of himself who dresses in the
latest Parisian styles without understanding the least bit about fashion.
Only one woman, Elaine, is Seinfeld's equal in wit, charm, and the
ability to play the game, but he can never realize it, fall in love with
her for any extended period of time, or promise to reform in order to
win her hand, because it would destroy the premise on which the
sitcom has achieved its great success. Only one woman, Harriet, is
Dorimant's equal in wit, charm, and the ability to play the game, and
when he realizes it, he falls in love with her and promises to reform
in order to win her hand, just as the play is ending.

What Seinfeld does, in program after program, is almost exactly
what Dorimant has done before him: make jokes, meet friends in res-
taurants, build a wardrobe, develop elaborate schemes to charm and
then break up with women, and, above all, preserve his freedom in

the face of the dangers and commitments of real love. Seinfeld, like Dorimant, cares more about his personal freedom than anything remotely like love. The primary difference between them is that Seinfeld is not always as successful as Dorimant in dealing with women, and that failure (which humanizes him) is what the sitcom plays for laughs. Trying to get one woman to break off with him because he has grown tired of her but does not want the guilt that would come if he broke off with her, Dorimant starts a complicated deception with her close friend, and although he does get in trouble with each of them because of it, he is able to carry it off and take her close friend as his lover. The male seducer in Etherege is successful, manipulative, and cruel. In a comparable moment on the sitcom, Seinfeld is carrying on an affair with a woman he has grown tired of, and suggests a ménage à trois with her roommate as a way of disgusting the first and charming the second. But the original woman finds the idea intriguing, and as the episode ends we see a startled look on Jerry's face. The male seducer on the sitcom is bungling rather than cruel. By recasting the calculating libertine as a neurotic comedian, *Seinfeld* turns the story about male strength into a story about male strength and weakness. Etherege's audience saw only men dumping women, but American television audiences are just as likely to see women dumping men.

Seinfeld is kinder and gentler than *The Man of Mode* in a number of respects. The sexual power struggles in the play are far more brutal and damaging than the comparable struggles on the sitcom, which seem more whimsically lighthearted than cruel. There is suffering in both stories, to be sure, but it seems more real and enduring in *The Man of Mode*. The characters are much friendlier to each other on the sitcom, helping each other out at all times of the day and night. Dorimant treats Sir Fopling Flutter with contempt and ridicule, and denounces his eccentricities; Jerry genuinely likes Kramer and accepts his weird behavior with few complaints. Along with this increase in compassion and fellow feeling, however, comes a concomitant decline in personal awareness and responsibility. When Dorimant dumps one woman and betrays another, they do not go away quietly, but remain on the stage, denouncing him at length and suffering in front of him. When Seinfeld breaks up with women, they typically have one or two lines of angry insult or scornful contempt and disappear forever. We don't see the dark side of the comedy as we do in Etherege. Dorimant is forced to think about his own behavior, and the women, in their conversations with each other, begin to understand how they have been victimized. There are many fewer moments of recognition on *Seinfeld*, in large measure because the characters cannot grow or change too much without destroying the premise of the program. And so Jerry continues to break off with women because they eat peas one at a time, or have male hands or closets full of birth-control sponges, but Dorimant can admit that he finds women boring or too clinging after he has seduced them.

The most striking revision of *The Man of Mode,* however, concerns the nearly total absence of moral characters in the sitcom, an alteration that allows *Seinfeld* to celebrate the victory of the neurotic and zany in ways that the Restoration comedy could never achieve. Contrasted with Dorimant and the others in *The Man of Mode* are two thoroughly moral and conventional lovers, Young Bellair and Emelia, who marry in the course of the play and affirm values of constancy, sincerity, and devotion. Dorimant and Medley think they are fools, and although they are not the primary focus of the action, they provide a continuing contrast with the value systems of the other characters—a kind of moral subplot. But unlike the other characters in the Etherege play, Young Bellair and Emelia are never funny, and perhaps for that reason characters like them are not part of the ongoing plot or character dynamic on *Seinfeld* except for one inspired single episode. Elaine meets mirror images of Jerry, George, and Kramer, earnest men who are kind, generous, and good, and who speak to each other with love and respect. Elaine toys with the idea of taking up with them and discarding her old friends, but realizes before it is too late that she belongs with the slobs. She is one of them. *Seinfeld* is *The Man of Mode* without the complications of moral seriousness.

Days of Our Lives

Television soap opera is an extremely variable melodramatic form capable of taking on the characteristics of a number of different popular genres, from mystery and science fiction to exotic adventure and Gothic horror, but it also replicates much more critically esteemed literary genres, including the great Jacobean revenge tragedies of seventeenth-century England. The particular episodes of the daytime soap opera *Days of Our Lives* considered here closely resemble two of the best of these revenge tragedies, John Webster's *White Devil* (1613) and *The Duchess of Malfi* (1623). These episodes of *Days of Our Lives* are *The Duchess of Malfi* or *The White Devil* with commercials, a soap opera that reworks virtually all of the conventions of the Jacobean form, adapting them to the demands of serial television production. The soap opera may be less aesthetically pure as a result, a kind of industrial art in the age of television, but the basic features of the story remain the same: the complex plots of intrigue, betrayal, murder, and revenge. An obsession with revenge drives the plots of Jacobean tragedy, just as it drives the plots of these episodes of *Days of Our Lives*, although the action is now presented in terms of ordinary life rather than in the grandiose theatrics of the Renaissance theater. More naturalistic in its settings, costumes, and language, the soap opera is Jacobean in its character types, actions, and themes. More talk may envelop the action, but the action itself remains what it was in seventeenth-century England.

Television soap opera is grounded in current events, and story lines on *Days of Our Lives* have revolved around a child trapped in an abandoned oil well, an AIDS-like epidemic, and a character who resembles Howard Hughes. Despite contemporary surface details, however, these particular episodes of the soap opera are Jacobean in content. At the same time their structure is remarkably similar to the compositional technique that Henry Fielding mastered in *Tom Jones* (1749), an elaborate pattern of close repetitions designed to teach eighteenth-century readers wit and judgment, what we might now describe as the ability to understand complex moral situations. The soap opera presents complex moral situations to its viewers in a manner very closely related to Fielding's. *Days of Our Lives* is a complex aesthetic achievement for precisely the same reasons that *The Duchess of Malfi*, *The White Devil*, and *Tom Jones* are: because it explores imaginatively and creatively, and with great care and precision, fundamental human drives, fears, and relationships.

The dukes, duchesses, cardinals, and their various retainers in Webster's plays have become the businessmen, lawyers, doctors, and their various retainers in the soap opera, but their essential natures and their relationships with each other have not changed significantly. Overcome by greed, sexual desire, and selfishness, these characters disregard morality, common sense, and the law to do whatever they want. Powerful and corrupt men struggle against each other, dominating most of the story; malcontents, cynics, and spies gather around them to do their dirty work; women try to be their equals but are most often their victims; and what simple but good-hearted souls remain are destroyed in one way or another by all the treachery that surrounds them. In Webster's tragedies these characters belong to one or two aristocratic Italian families torn apart by hatred, lust, and hypocrisy; in *Days of Our Lives* they belong to two or three middle-class American families torn apart by nearly identical passions. There are numerous imprisonments, abductions, threats, trials, intruders, poisoners, and almost continual suffering and pain in both kinds of stories. Characters search for meaningful love in spite of these dangers, but emotional commitment is extremely difficult to achieve or maintain. Family and the other institutions of society are corrupted and prove unable to sustain normal human life in the face of the power of the egotistical psychopaths.

The prostitute Vittoria Corombona begins a sexual liaison with the powerful duke of Brachiano in *The White Devil*, aided by her brother, the cynical and mocking malcontent Flamineo, while their good-hearted mother watches helplessly as her children sink into villainy. At Vittoria's urging, the duke has Vittoria's husband's neck broken and his own wife poisoned by means of a powder sprinkled on a picture of the duke that she is in the custom of kissing. Although there is an arrest and a trial, no one is ever brought to justice for these crimes. The brutal murders initiate a complex revenge plot in which many others are poisoned, tortured, or otherwise butchered, and by the end of the play nearly everybody is dead. The pattern is repeated in *The Duchess of Malfi*, where a wealthy and powerful duke joins with his brother, a cardinal, to keep their recently widowed sister, the duchess of Malfi, from marrying again. When she disobeys them and secretly marries her steward, risking all for the chance of personal happiness, they have her brutally strangled by their spy, Bosola, another cynical and mocking malcontent. The torture and murder of the duchess initiates another complex revenge plot as Bosola turns on the duke, and by the end of the play most of the other characters are poisoned, tortured, or otherwise butchered, some in spectacular fashion.

Virtually all of this reappears on *Days of Our Lives*. Of the various story lines that alternate with each other on the soap opera in a single

three-month period, the most murderous (and Jacobean) concerns
Lawrence Alamain, a rich and powerful businessman who is murdering undercover police agents in the community of Salem with vials of
a deadly HIV-like virus. A cynical and mocking malcontent who
laughs at his adversaries when he is not otherwise trying to kill them,
Alamain defies the ability of law enforcement to bring him to justice.
When undercover female police agent Kimberly Brady (formerly a
prostitute) pretends to fall in love with him in order to get important
evidence, one of his henchmen tries to poison her, but she is saved at
the last minute by her ex-husband, Shane Donovan. Meanwhile Kimberly's sister Kayla, who holds Alamain responsible for the murder of
her husband, urges her family to take its own private revenge on him.
Eventually Alamain is arrested and brought to trial, not for these murders, however, but for the rape of another woman, Jennifer Horton.
At the trial, his lawyer accuses the community of "misguided revenge"
against capitalism.

This is *The White Devil* in modern dress. Alamain is a brilliant
combination of the murderous and powerful duke and the mocking
and cynical malcontent, and Kimberly is a new version of the prostitute Vittoria who plays a dangerous game with him. Like the duke,
Alamain kills almost casually and is vulnerable to the charms of a
prostitute. Like the malcontent Flamineo, he is an outsider who considers himself above the law and makes fun of everyone around him.
And like the prostitute Vittoria, Kimberly quickly becomes involved
in complex intrigues that scare those who really care for her. Kimberly's mother, like Vittoria's mother before her, watches in horror as
her daughter becomes involved with the evil man. And although there
are important trials in both stories, no one is ever brought to justice.

A second story line on the soap opera concerns another rich and
powerful businessman, Victor Kiriakis, a villain who prevents his recently widowed son Bo from marrying the woman he loves, Dr. Carly
Manning, with the help of forged letters and a spy, Emmy Borden.
Carly renounces Bo and marries Kiriakis, but when Emmy turns on
Kiriakis and tries to poison Carly, Bo drinks it instead and almost
dies, and Kiriakis has Emmy brutally murdered. This is *The Duchess
of Malfi* in modern dress: Kiriakis is a new version of the duke, a
powerful and hateful man who wants to stop a woman he loves from
marrying a rival, employs a spy to get what he wants, and finally
orders the murder of a woman. Emmy is a new version of the spy, a

character who first does the powerful man's dirty business and then turns against him. And Carly is a new version of the duchess of Malfi, a good but confused woman, out of place in a world of self-serving manipulators and, in fact, also a princess who has come to Salem to try to be an ordinary person. Just as the duchess finds brief moments of love and happiness with the man she marries, her household steward who is well beneath her in rank, so does the princess in her relationship with Bo, who is also beneath her in rank.

The principal technique by which the writers of *Days of Our Lives* multiply content, setting up precise patterns of repetition between characters and events, is comparable to the ways in which Henry Fielding devised his great novel *Tom Jones* in the middle of the eighteenth century. Forced to solve a problem nearly identical to that faced by the writers of television soap opera—how to enlarge the simple plots of the drama to the longer forms demanded by the new style of storytelling that he called the comic epic—Fielding took the characters and events of the comic drama he knew, within which some repetitions between main plot and subplot often take place, and repeated these many more times over. Each time he made subtle changes in these repetitions, duplicating and triplicating character and incident in a way that required his readers to distinguish the differences between them. The result was the first great comic novel in English, an immense and intricate architectonic structure of repetition and a brilliant adaptation of the eighteenth-century concepts of wit and judgment, the one the ability to see similarity within difference, the other the ability to see difference within similarity. These together constituted wisdom for the eighteenth century, and *Tom Jones* is a novel designed to teach its readers that kind of discrimination. *Days of Our Lives* does exactly the same thing in almost exactly the same way and for almost exactly the same reason: the need to turn the shorter dramatic form into something ongoing and much longer—the melodramatic epic.

Parallel actions within the soap opera's plot lines invite both viewers and the characters themselves to consider similarity and difference as cameras move back and forth between couples who are embracing, couples who are making love, or couples who are discussing their failure to consummate relationships. Each individual involved in the identical action is different in some essential way, either good or bad, sincere or insincere, confused or clear-headed, and from these differences a whole series of complex contrasts are set up, which are foregrounded by the program. An episode in which one couple argues about trust and deception is almost immediately followed by two or three other episodes in which different characters in different relationships say virtually the same things to each other. Sometimes the meanings of these words change in each context, demonstrating a kind of moral flexibility, but sometimes they do not. The viewer is asked quite explicitly to compare and contrast. A man gives a woman a piece of jewelry that was his mother's, and a moment later another man does the same to her sister. Because the first man is a Machiavellian manipulator and a murderer his gift is immediately suspect, and because the second man is a good police agent out to arrest him, his gift is not. But the soap opera highlights other aspects of the presentation that ask viewers for greater powers of discrimination than that. The woman to whom the murderer offers his mother's pin is the policeman's ex-wife, and she remembers when her husband gave her his mother's pin. The woman to whom the police agent gives his mother's ring is now his ex-wife's sister, who is torn by her love for the man and her love for her sister. In a world in which everyone is morally compromised it is not possible to see one action as good and sincere and one as bad and insincere; the story asks its viewers to discriminate. This is not mindless repetition in order to generate content, but a method of storytelling that presents real challenges to its audience.

This kind of patterning of complex repetition can be seen most clearly in the Kiriakis plot. Kiriakis and Carly Manning embrace in their bedroom after their wedding, but she is deeply troubled about Bo and will not allow Kiriakis any sexual intimacy. Bo and Emmy are shown embracing at the same time, in Bo's bedroom, but Bo is deeply troubled about Carly and will not allow Emmy any sexual intimacy. The camera moves back and forth between the two couples in such a way that it is often impossible to tell which character is in view. As Emmy begins undressing, Bo pulls back, and then there is a quick camera switch and we see that it is in fact Victor who is undressing and Carly who is pulling back. A short time later Kiriakis is shown buying a special dress for Carly to wear to his birthday party, and at the store they meet Bo and Emmy, who are involved in an identical errand. Victor tells Carly that she looks beautiful, but then Bo tells Carly, rather than Emmy, the same, and when they move on to another room Emmy hacks up the dress Carly has just purchased.

At their best, these complex patterns of repetitions ask viewers to make moral judgments. At the same time that Shane must lie to Kayla about his police activities with Kimberly because the police prevent him from telling her anything about their plot to trap Alamain, Kimberly must lie to Alamain, pretending to have strong positive feelings for him. Somewhat uneasy about her behavior, Alamain repeatedly asks Kimberly to reassure him that she will never deceive him, at the same time that Kayla makes identical requests of Shane. Shane comforts Kayla by bringing her tea; Kimberly comforts Alamain by stroking him maternally. Both are lying for the same cause, but one of those suffering is good and undeserving of the deceit, the other bad and deserving. Does that or can that justify either deception? The soap does not say but leads viewers to the clearly and explicitly framed question. This is exactly how the Fielding novel operates. And at culminating moments of the plot the characters themselves learn moral judgment from understanding these very same patterns of repetition.

For us too, the truth comes from following the patterns of repetition, not only those within the soap opera, but those between the soap opera and the older form of Jacobean revenge tragedy. Those parallels are profound.

CHAPTER 6

Tragedy, the ENQUIRER, and the Critics

The National Enquirer, People, and the other supermarket tabloids and gossip magazines publishing on their models are contemporary versions of tragedy—Euripides, Ibsen, or Strindberg rewritten according to the demands of the American marketplace. Preoccupied with the rise and fall of media celebrities—but primarily with the fall, and thus filled with stories of suffering, ruin, error, self-knowledge, recovery, and death—publications such as the *Enquirer* reproduce much of the traditional content of tragedy although in greatly abridged and fragmented forms: "Liz Tragedy: The Secret Life She Hides from the World" (*Enquirer*, June 4, 1996, cover); "Jack Lord's Tragic Last Days" (*Enquirer*, September 17, 1996, cover). *People* is less crassly sensational, interested in the rise as well as the fall and in the recovery after the fall, but it is otherwise quite similar: "Ennis Cosby's Murder: A Family in Pain" (*People*, February 3, 1997, cover); "Margot Kidder: Back from Hell" (*People*, September 23, 1996, cover); "The Last Days of Ryan White: . . . The Final Hours of the Boy Whose Battle with AIDS Touched America's Heart" (*People*, April 23, 1990, cover).

These are stories about many different kinds of suffering and fall, and although they are not complete tragedies as Aristotle, Nietzsche, or most contemporary literary critics would define them, they are the dramatic turning points of tragedies or would-be tragedies and fit many of the most important critical definitions of tragedy and the tragic. "The story of tragedy, then, is the change from prosperity to adversity, determined by the general and external fact of mutability," Chaucer wrote in "The Monk's Tale." Sidney wrote that tragedy "teachest the uncertainty of this world, and upon how weake foundations guilden roofes are builded." But even by much more detailed and restrictive contemporary definitions, the stories in supermarket tabloids and celebrity gossip magazines qualify as tragedy. "A tragedy is a final and impressive disaster due to an unforeseen or unrealized failure involving people who command respect and sympathy," Geoffrey Brereton explains in a typical contemporary discussion. "It often entails an ironical change of fortune and usually conveys a strong impression of waste. It is always accompanied by misery and emotional distress" (*Principles of Tragedy*, 20). These certainly are the characteristics of the stories in the *Enquirer* and *People*.

"Tragedy, for us, has been mainly the conflict between an individual and the forces that destroy him," Raymond Williams argues (*Modern Tragedy*, 87), and he lists as the primary elements of this genre "order and accident; the destruction of the hero; the irreparable action and its connections with death; and the emphasis on evil" (46). These, too, are all present in the tabloid form or the more refined magazine of celebrity gossip. "There is social tragedy: men destroyed by power and famine; a civilization destroyed or destroying itself," Williams explains. "And then there is personal tragedy: men and women suffering and destroyed in their closest relationships; the individual knowing his destiny, in a cold universe, in which death and an ultimate spiritual isolation are alternative forms of the same suffering and heroism" (121). This latter variant, personal rather than social, is the tragic vision of the gossip magazines and tabloids: "Hate Flourishes on the Street Where the Families of a Killer and His Victim Still Live" (*People*, April 30, 1990, 58); "James Brown Tried to Kill Me" (*Enquirer Special: Scandals of the Rich and Famous*, fall 1990, 19); "I Survived 90 Minutes in Tomb of Terror—Swept Away by a Sea of Sewage" (*Enquirer*, September 25, 1990, 24).

There are, of course, significant differences between the tabloids and the gossip magazines and traditional tragic literature—this is not, after all, Euripides, even if the story of Medea would be appropriate material for the *Enquirer*. If Camus was right to call tragedy "one of the rarest of flowers" ("Future of Tragedy," 298), then the *Enquirer* might be considered the peskiest of weeds. Perhaps the most important

difference is in the kind of intellectual demands made by these gossip
sheets; there is nothing like the inwardness or subjectivity of the individual that G. W. F. Hegel, Søren Kierkegaard, and the critics following them have insisted upon. And there is no literary language or
literary structure. In place of Friedrich Nietzsche's lyrical dithyrambs
we have only the most elementary and sensational of prose styles,
nothing at all akin to poetry. The tragic language that Camus called
for, "both hieratic and familiar, barbarous and learned, mysterious
and clear, haughty and pitiful" (307), is here only familiar, barbarous,
and clear. In place of the careful elaborations of character, theme, and
plot typical of literary tragedy there are now only a number of short,
discontinuous, and easy-to-read narratives following each other hap-
hazardly. But if the treatment of the story is much less literary, that
by itself should not make the content any less tragic. Walter Benjamin's statement that narration is replaced by information, and information by sensation, reflecting "the increasing atrophy of experience"
("On Some Motifs in Baudelaire," 159), is relevant here. The *Enquirer*
and *People* demonstrate such a shift from narration to information to
sensation, and if as atrophied versions of tragedy they are less coherent
than what has come before, they also seem appropriate for an age if
not of atrophied experience at least of fragmented experience. Pictures
replace text. Brereton speaks of "the dilution of tragedy in the past
hundred years or so" (279), and Williams—who describes "the tragic
voice" as "the aspiration for a meaning, at the very limits of man's
strength; the known meanings and answers, affirmed and yet also
questioned, broken down, by contradictory experience" (90)—
acknowledges that such a voice is now in decline.

What the *Enquirer* offers is just such a tragic voice in decline: "Liz's
Secrets Revealed in Best Pal's Diaries and We've Got Them All" (*En-
quirer*, September 24, 1996, cover); "Liz Tragedy: Legendary Beauty
Battles Age, Insomnia, & Loneliness . . . and Larry Wants $$ from Liz
to Sue Her" (*Enquirer*, June 4, 1996, 24); "Liz's Life on the Edge:
Scandal's Her Middle Name: she stole her pal's husband, fought
through 7 marriages, abused drugs and booze and pushed her sick
body to the limit" (*Enquirer Special: Scandals of the Rich and Famous*,
fall 1990, 66). What every reader of the *Globe*, the *Star*, and the *En-
quirer* knows is that this is a woman, once beautiful, who suffers from
despair, depression, chemical dependency, eating disorders, and a pas-
sion for men. She could be a character straight out of Euripides or

Strindberg. In the *Hippolytus* (428 B.C.) of Euripides, for example, Phaedra, a beautiful woman married to Theseus, the king of Athens, is overcome by her passion for her stepson, Hippolytus. Refusing to break the sexual code of behavior and act on her feelings, she hides away in her palace and starves herself. The chorus notes sadly that her beauty is fading fast, while her nurse tries to figure out what has gone wrong. The play, which is as much about Hippolytus's renunciation of sexuality as it is about Phaedra's passion, shows us the destruction that results when Hippolytus learns about his stepmother's feelings and savagely denounces her. Humiliated, Phaedra commits suicide but not before leaving a note behind that claims that Hippolytus has raped her, which causes Theseus to order his son put to death. At the very end of the play, as his son dies painfully in front of him, Theseus learns what really has happened in a moving recognition scene. It is too late for anything except understanding and forgiveness, attitudes Euripides is interested in developing in his audiences as well, since he elaborates a series of fairly long and carefully articulated speeches, meditations, and debates on the nature of passion and the ways in which it complicates and even destroys our lives. The *Enquirer*'s version of the life of Elizabeth Taylor is not nearly as complex, but the basic materials are all there except for the death of the heroine—but we all know that the *Enquirer* has been on a kind of macabre death watch.

As it is played out in the tabloids, Taylor's life also resembles more recent tragedy. In August Strindberg's play *Miss Julie* (1888), a spoiled aristocratic young woman is overcome by her sexual passion for a servant and, unlike Phaedra, she does break the sexual code of behavior with him, although just once. The play shows us the destruction that results. Julie is humiliated at having crossed the lines of sex and class and is ready to commit suicide, although the play stops before the action is complete, as the servant urges her to kill herself. The recognition scenes are much more limited and there are fewer speeches about the nature of passion. Strindberg is more interested in showing than telling. A century later, in the tragedy portrayed in the *Enquirer* we find Elizabeth Taylor overcome by her sexual passion, along with her desire for drugs and alcohol. Then, in a series of fragments, each shorter than *Miss Julie*, the tabloid shows us some of the destruction that results or may result: the increasingly frail and sickly woman on the ropes, in and out of hospitals, gaining weight, losing weight, gaining weight, marrying a man below her in class and then divorcing him. There are only the smallest moments of recognition now and no speeches at all about passion. Euripides, Strindberg, and the *Enquirer* constitute a progression of the tragic form.

What *People* offers is a somewhat different version of this kind of tragedy, not only in its stories of suffering and fall on the model of the *Enquirer* but also in its stories of suffering and fall that end in recovery. The comparable story about Elizabeth Taylor in *People* is "At Long Last Liz. She is back among us. After her toughest fight yet against pain and addiction, the unsinkable Liz Taylor comes home to a tearful salute from Hollywood—with a lot of help from her friends" (*People*, March 13, 1989, cover). Like the bourgeois tragedy of the eighteenth and nineteenth centuries with its tacked-on happy endings, *People*'s tragedy is often irrepressibly upbeat in this fashion. The suffering and the fall are still there, but are now patched up in the ending. "Sexy, Saucy, Outrageous Cybill Shepherd" (*People*, October 8, 1990, cover) is yet another replay of the *Miss Julie* situation, another story of a woman who is overcome by sexual passion, breaks the codes of behavior, and suffers heartache because of it, but where the *Enquirer* would play the story as a fall, *People* plays it as a rise: "*Moonlighting*'s over, and so are her two marriages. Now at 40 she's taking a gamble by making *Texasville* with ex-lover Peter Bogdanovich. So what's she got? Three great kids, a new boyfriend, and no regrets." This is an important difference between *People* and the *Enquirer*: although both are drawn to stories of suffering and fall, *People* prefers stories of recovery. The *Enquirer* does not. *People* becomes a less embarrassing kind of text in contemporary culture, less a dark threat to the harmony of the status quo, and is therefore appropriate to doctors' waiting rooms; the *Enquirer* remains virtually untouchable in polite society. Devoted to the "lurid truth" hidden from polite society, the *Enquirer* shows the destruction of all our idols.

In spite of their different emphases, publications such as *People* and the *Enquirer* can be seen as the latest stage in the long and distinguished history of tragedy. Thus the *Enquirer* story "Father Kills Himself to Get Revenge from beyond the Grave: My evil Dad framed me for his murder" (September 18, 1990, 12) repeats elements of the suicide of Phaedra, who falsely blames Hippolytus for raping her. In the same issue the *Enquirer* story "After Eight Years Together and Three Kids, Horrified Wife Discovers: 'I Married My Father' " (September

18, 1990, 5) repeats obvious elements of the Oedipus story. The story in the *Globe* "Grace's Curse Strikes Caroline. She had a horrible premonition husband would die in accident. They fought bitterly the night before he died when he refused her tearful plea to quit race" (*Globe*, October 23, 1990, cover) repeats the oracle's curse on the house of Atreus in *The Oresteia*. "Laid on the family about 1297 by a woman who was kidnapped by Rainier I" and who is reported to have proclaimed, "Never will a Grimaldi find true happiness in marriage," the curse has been remarkably effective. The *Globe* lists all the Grimaldis so cursed and destroyed and then explains the attempts of the current Grimaldis to fight against their fate. It is an impressive tale of death and destruction.

The *Enquirer* and *People* are not pure tragedy, and their dominant tragic content is presented against several counterthemes that work to ameliorate what would otherwise be an overwhelming preoccupation with suffering. In the *Enquirer* this takes the form of stories about the success of ordinary people in extraordinary situations: "Great-Granny, 83, Shoots Berserk Burglar to Death . . . He Was Battering Down Bedroom Door" (*Enquirer*, April 10, 1990); "No Hands or Feet, but He Bowls, Dances and Plays Drums in a Band" (*Enquirer*, February 6, 1990). *People* is full of more ordinary kinds of gossip about celebrities, pictures of them at parties, at play, and at work, and, unlike the *Enquirer*, is more likely to be filled with other stories that are closer to the contents of the mainline news magazines. Tabloids and gossip magazines are also obviously melodramatic, and my claim that they are contemporary variants of tragedy is not meant to deny these important elements. Of all the characteristics of melodrama listed by Peter Brooks in *The Melodramatic Imagination*, "the indulgence of strong emotionalism; moral polarization and schematizations; extreme states of being, situations, actions; overt villainy, persecution of the good, and final reward of virtue; inflated and extravagant expression; dark plottings, suspense, breathtaking peripety" (12–13), most of which can be found in the tabloids and gossip magazines, the most important is the "inflated and extravagant expression" of their descriptive vocabularies.

But in spite of these important melodramatic elements, it is tragedy that is the dominant genre: "Richard Pryor in Betty Ford Clinic after Wild Coke Binge: If I Don't Beat Coke This Time, I'm Just Going to Wind Up Dead" (*Enquirer*, February 6, 1990, 7). The language is melodramatic but the story is tragic, concerned as it is with Pryor's self-knowledge and with his internal conflict. "I'm as far down in the barrel as you can get," he is quoted in the story as saying. "I'm really afraid I won't be able to climb out this time. If I don't straighten my life out, I'm going to end up in the gutter, penniless like some old bum. I don't want that to happen—but I don't know how to stop it." In tragedy, Robert Heilman argues, an individual is torn by the urgency of his "unreconciled impulses"; in melodrama the conflict takes place between individuals. The *Enquirer* story presents the urgency of Pryor's unreconciled impulses and shows his internal conflicts, for Pryor has been a media success in part because he has so brilliantly flouted conventional morality and made that the subject of his comic monologues. The *Enquirer* reports, "He's spent his 49 years racing along life's fast lane. His drug and alcohol abuse, public fights and five broken marriages have earned the brilliant funnyman a reputation as one of Hollywood's wild men." Only after he caught on fire free-basing cocaine did white audiences begin to come to his concerts in large numbers, performances that used the incident as a primary sub-ject for comic elaboration. That what has made his rise would also make his fall, and that he would recognize all this, however briefly, in the process of the fall, is the stuff of tragedy. "On one side we have moral ordinance, on the other the unruly passion," Heilman explains. "The imperative is the voice of tradition and community, the impulse is the egotism, the appetite or fever or rage, any private urgency that runs counter to restrictions" (*Tragedy and Melodrama*, 11). Here, too, the *Enquirer's* treatment of the Pryor story fits what Heilman claims is the essential defining characteristic of the tragic. " 'I haven't learned a thing since I set myself on fire in 1980 and nearly died,' he told fellow addicts at the clinic. 'I suffered burns all over my body then and went through excruciating agony, yet drugs still have me in a deadly grip I can't shake.' " Pryor knows he is violating a moral or-dinance with his own unruly passion, at least as the *Enquirer* presents it, and what we are asked to understand is the private urgency that runs counter to restrictions. By other standards, too, the *Enquirer's* treatment of Pryor is predominantly tragic. Pryor himself closely re-sembles the Dionysian satyr that Nietzsche placed at the center of tragic action, the "ecstatic reveler" and "symbol of the sexual omnip-otence of nature" that threatens all who are timorous: "Confronted with him, the man of culture shriveled into a mendacious caricature"

("Birth of Tragedy," 61). Yet the *Enquirer*'s treatment of Pryor highlights the fact that he is, finally, just a man like the rest of us, not a superman. Pryor's self-knowledge also fits Hegel's insistence on personal freedom.

People produces a very similar sort of condensed tragic story: "Halston, 1932–1990. He put American fashion on the map. He dressed Jackie, Liz and Liza. He died last week of AIDS, a broken man" (*People*, April 9, 1990). What made Halston a success, we are told, was his willingness to be on the cutting edge of fashion, to live as a member of the avant garde, but that was also finally responsible for his personal destruction. *People* shows us photographs of Halston during the time of his great success, when he lived as a part of the circle of Andy Warhol, Liza Minelli, and Liz Taylor, flouting the rules with them, indulging in what the magazine describes as "drugs and debauchery." Then we are treated to the story of the fall itself, Halston's illness and death. In tragedy, Albert Camus writes, a man comes into conflict with the divine order "personified by a god or incarnated in society" because of a desire for power, a sense of pride, or simply because of his own stupidity ("Future of Tragedy," 302). Casting the life of Halston into this model, we produce such a man, his desire for power, his fall on account of pride and stupidity, and his conflict with a social order. The order is no longer divine and the man no longer has the stature of Prometheus, but what Hegel has characterized as the tragic collision remains. At the center of liberal tragedy, Raymond Williams writes, is "a man at the height of his powers and the limits of his strength, at once aspiring and being defeated, releasing and destroyed by his own energies" (*Modern Tragedy*, 87). This is Halston's tragedy as presented to us by *People*, although at the center of the tragedy of mass society now is not a great reformer, a hero from Ibsen, but rather a successful fashion designer who wanted to succeed and to be admired by society.

Definitions of Tragedy

How well does tabloid tragedy fit the extensive critical literature about tragedy? By how many definitions are the stories in the *Enquirer* and *People* really tragedy? Tragedy, William McCollom writes, "encourages a metaphysical frame of mind, a concern with the broadest possible questions. . . . 'What kind of world do we live in? How are we

to judge man's life?' " (*Tragedy*, 8). These are also the preoccupations
of the *Enquirer* and *People*, although they are now answered in terms
of the lives of media celebrities. Questions about the kind of world we
live in, about the ways we are to judge a man's or a woman's life,
about whether an individual's values are those of the world, are constantly raised by the *Enquirer, People*, and the other tabloids on their
model: "Vanna! Ex-roommate reveals her dark, shocking secrets. 6
months as Wayne Newton's mistress. How she lost weight—using
cocaine. The X rated home video that could destroy her career" (*Enquirer*, February 6, 1990). Such scandal-mongering is not metaphysical in the usual sense, but it does raise McCollom's questions
about values, judgments, and ethics. And although the headlines imply
that Vanna White is guilty—a scheming little adventuress, to use the
language of melodrama—the story that follows tells us that she was
physically abused by an early boyfriend, complicating the issue of guilt
and responsibility. By what standards, then, are we to judge this individual? McCollom's questions—What kind of world do we live in?
How are we to judge man's life?—are also the *Enquirer*'s questions.
And if, as he argues, these are metaphysical concerns, then the *Enquirer* is metaphysical. Max Scheler argues that "the quality of the
tragic is lacking when the question 'Who is guilty?' has a clear and
definite answer. Only where no such answer can be given does the
stuff of tragedy begin to appear" ("On the Tragic," 13), and here in
the story about Vanna White no such answer can be given. She is a
victim first, but then a violator of moral norms. "Something draws me
to men who treat me rough," she is quoted as saying (*Enquirer*, February 6, 1990, 37).

One might object that this is to take celebrity gossip much too seriously, to confuse trash with literature, and to assist in the destruction
of standards of taste and judgment. The scandal-mongering nature of
the tabloids would appear to deny all claims to seriousness, except, of
course, that specific tales of specific celebrities do illustrate general
conditions of human behavior. If we can see Medea as a mythic figure,
she belongs in tragedy; when we see her as a specific and altogether
trivial celebrity, she belongs only in the *Enquirer*. There are other
significant objections, however. The ephemeral nature of the tabloids
would appear to deny any claim to permanent and transcendent value,
except that these stories vary very little, week by week or year by year.
The names change but the stories remain the same, and what may first

appear topical is much more permanent and transcendent. Once prejudice against the topical can be put aside, moreover, important similarities between the content of the tabloids and the content of traditional literature can be seen.

Against a wide range of discussions of tragedy as an attitude, publications such as the *Enquirer* fit rather closely: a concern with ancient evil, self-destruction, incompatible human needs, the permanence and mystery of suffering. The tabloids are preoccupied with despair of this sort. "The tragic vision," William Sewall writes, "sees man as questioner, naked, unaccommodated, alone, facing mysterious, demonic forces in his own nature and outside, and the irreducible facts of suffering and death" (*Vision of Tragedy*, 4, 5). The tabloids certainly see man as a fornicator, naked and unsatisfied, but also as questioner, naked and unaccommodated. Along with the articles about adulterers, the "inside stories of big-money divorces, royal love romps, sex in high society, . . . star studs and gays" (*Enquirer Special: Scandals of the Rich and Famous*, fall 1990, cover), tabloids and gossip magazines also present us with articles like "The Haunting Last Days of Jim Henson. . . . The gentle genius who gave us Kermit and the Muppets was unsparing of himself. He ignored the infection ravaging his body until it was too late. 'Maybe I'm dying,' he said . . ." (*People*, June 18, 1990, cover). Here is man naked, unaccommodated, alone, facing destructive forces and the irreducible facts of suffering and death. And if Henson is not shown here to be very much of a questioner, *People* itself takes on that role in the manner of its presentation of the case.

Tragedy as literary form is more problematic since these fragments lack the traditional elaborations of literature, and yet again and again we are presented with incompatible needs locked in dramatic combat, with protagonists heightened and intensified, with good and bad canceling each other out, with great figures made little by what opposes them, and with struggle within which there is mental, emotional, and moral growth and then exhaustion. Aristotle's description of the various characteristics of Greek tragedy provides an obvious standard against which the tabloids can be evaluated as well. The tragic fable of the tabloid is incomplete, lacking beginning, middle, or end, but only if a single issue of the *Enquirer* or *People* is taken as the text. Read as tragedy in weekly installments, however, the ongoing saga of Elizabeth Taylor or other celebrities does approach the structure of traditional storytelling. Many of the other elements of tragedy that Aristotle prized so highly are also present in the tabloid form. There is often irony (reversal in the course of events, in accordance with the rules of probability and necessity), disclosure (the change from ignorance to self-knowledge), and crisis of feeling (the harmful or painful experience at the heart of the story). Thus the story titled "*Dallas Star's Booze-Soaked Nightmare:* 'I was the king of skid-row bars. I guzzled a fifth of vodka and 12 beers each day' " (*Enquirer*, September 18, 1990, 6) includes the fall into alcoholism, the recognition of error, and the disaster that forces a change in behavior. Of the various changes in fortune that Aristotle considers, he rejects two as inappropriate for tragedy: decent people passing from good fortune to misfortune, and vicious people passing from misfortune to good fortune. Neither is morally suitable to tragedy. Here, too, the tabloids follow Aristotle's injunctions, and apparently the same basic morality still applies. For tragedy, Aristotle requires an individual between these extremes, neither entirely virtuous nor entirely base, who fails not because of innate evil but because of error. The characters of the *Enquirer* and *People* are subject to such Aristotelian errors of judgment, which precipitate disaster. The issue of pity and fear is harder to consider because it raises complex issues of reader response, but certainly the contents of the *Enquirer* are a litany of common fears. A typical issue of the *Enquirer* contains stories about miscarriage, AIDS, cancer, drug addiction, infidelity, and, for toppers, the problems of falling into an open sewer, not all of which require that the victims have made an error. Because we are shown individuals experiencing each of these catastrophes, the claim can certainly be made that the *Enquirer* is manipulating both our pity and our fear.

Other objections to the tabloids as tragedy can be made. "Where there is no sense of the infinite vastness of what is beyond our grasp," Karl Jaspers argues, "all we finally succeed in conveying is misery— not tragedy. This is the peculiar predicament of modern tragedy since the Enlightenment" ("Basic Characteristics," 47). Following Jaspers, who would deny the possibility of modern tragedy in this way, it is easy enough to see tabloids such as the *Enquirer* as texts only of such modern misery, and yet here, too, albeit in abbreviated form, the *Enquirer* also contains a sense of the infinite vastness beyond our grasp in its horoscopes and its numerous tales of religious and sometimes of supernatural miracle and intervention: "Man Refuses to Buy House after Owner Admits It's Haunted—& Loses $32,000" (*Enquirer*, April 10, 1990, 19); "Amazing! All Five of Reader's Predictions Came True" (*Enquirer*, February 6, 1990, 43); "Friends Born at the Same Time and Place Suddenly Die on Same Day" *(Enquirer*, February 6, 1990, 11). The last article includes the following statement: "I feel it must be some kind of destiny. God had a hand in this. They came into the world almost at the same time—and God called them home almost at the same time."

Tabloids in the History of Tragedy

Larger issues remain about the meaning and importance of this new form of tragedy. None of this is *King Lear*, but it may be the appropriate literature for an age raised on television. We might even call it postmodern tragedy, an extravagant, minimalist celebration of the death of the subject made available in collage or montage form, to sound for a minute like a postmodern critic. If "collage is the single most revolutionary formal innovation in artistic representation to occur in our century," as Gregory Ulmer asserts ("Object of Post-Criticism," 84), then we should have collage tragedy. The tragic literature based on Athenian or Elizabethan models of the individual has given way to the tragic literature based on poststructuralist models that reject the concept of the individual as a myth. The *Enquirer* is contemporaneous with the poststructualists and confirms them. To paraphrase Robert Venturi's call for a postmodern architecture, *Learning from Las Vegas*, this is literature that has already learned from Las Vegas, and it is perhaps no accident that many of the celebrities whose lives make up the tragedy of the tabloids are themselves Las Vegas entertainers. "There is no important tragedy, within the Christian world, until there is also humanism and indeed individualism," Williams argues (*Modern Tragedy*, 88), and Suzanne Langer writes that "tragedy can arise and flourish only where people are aware of individual life as an end in itself, and as a measure of other things" ("Great Dramatic Forms," 354). What follows the loss of belief in the individual man or woman is not necessarily the death of tragedy but only its reappearance in a form appropriate to new economic and cultural conditions.

The tragic lives of celebrities have come to replace the tragic lives of the mythic figures of ancient Greece. Elizabeth Taylor, driven by her passion, and suffering because of it, replaces Phaedra from Euripides' *Hippolytus*. Both disintegrate in front of us, one more quickly than the other. And just as the action of Greek tragedy is the history of ruling families, the action of tabloid tragedy is the history of the Kennedy family, the British royal family, the Onassis family, and whatever other families are currently newsworthy. Mythic families stand between ordinary men and the gods. Celebrities are now similarly situated.

But where there once was rising and falling action, a beginning, a middle, and an end, extensive discussion of thematic meanings, and a group of interrelated characters, there is now only Taylor's life as it is reported over time in successive issues of the tabloids, mixed up now with the fragments of the lives of other unrelated characters, among them Ryan White, a teenager who has died from AIDS, Joel Steinberg, a lawyer convicted of killing his child, and Jimmy Swaggart, a preacher revealed as an adulterer and hypocrite. But these individuals replace familiar tragic figures that we have met before: Oswald Alving, the character from Ibsen's *Ghosts* dying from a sexually transmitted (or inherited) disease, Medea, the child killer from Euripides, and Tartuffe, the preacher/adulterer from Molière's tragicomic *Tartuffe*. The *Enquirer* article previously mentioned, "After 8 Years Together and 3 Kids, Horrified Wife Discovers: 'I Married My Father'," repeats Oedipus, just as all the assorted astrologers who appear in the tabloids with their uncanny ability to predict doom for the kingdom echo Tiresias. We are in a great chaos of tragic characters and tragic themes, the raw materials from which, in the past, great drama has been created, only now we have no drama. Whereas the great tragic or tragicomic playwrights of the past made connections for us by developing coherent themes and structures, the tabloids only present characters in search of authors, fragments of many different tragic stories presented without structure. If sense is to be made of them, then, it must come from the active participation of the reader, who is encouraged, however, only to experience them as discontinuous fragments.

Distinguishing tragedy, the literary form, from the tragic vision, Murray Krieger writes, "The tragic vision remains what it was, but it can no longer be made through tragedy to yield to an order and a shared religious vision. The ultimately absorbent power of tragedy, symbolic of the earned affirmation of universals, is gone" (*Tragic Vi-*

sion, 17). For Krieger what follows is "the modernism that is characterized by fragmentation" rather than synthesis (6), and although
he was not writing about the *Enquirer*, he could have been. But nothing wanders free of its own history, and the tabloids are necessarily
confined within the developments of tragedy as genre. That history as
it is traced by Williams approaches its modern form with romanticism,
and it is here that the fundamental characteristics of the tabloids can
clearly be seen, especially in what Williams describes as the devious
and perverse desires of Faust. "The desires of man are again intense
and imperative; they reach out and test the universe itself. Society is
identified as convention, and convention is the enemy of desire." Desire becomes devious in romanticism and revolt becomes a defiance of
convention and morality. "There is a related preoccupation with remorse: deep, pervasive, and beyond all its nominal causes. For in Romantic Tragedy man is guilty of the ultimate and nameless crime of
being himself" (*Modern Tragedy*, 94). Thus the *Enquirer* gives us
"Untold stories behind the sexcapades that toppled top evangelists
from their gilded pulpits: Their Gospel was lust and greed. Baker's
Gay Lover tells all; Swaggart trysts with prostitutes and Noriega"
(*Enquirer Special: Scandals of the Rich and Famous*, fall 1990, 30).
We are back to the Faust legend.

Williams argues that after romanticism, tragedy splits into public
and private versions, the first typified by Ibsen, the second by Strindberg and O'Neill. In public tragedy the romantic outcast becomes the
individual liberator who tries to transform the world, whereas in private tragedy the romantic outcast is an isolated figure who desires and
fights alone. The supermarket tabloids belong within this second tradition—Williams calls it "the tragedy of destructive relationships"—
along with the plays of Strindberg, O'Neill, and Tennessee Williams,
in which "men and women seek to destroy each other in the act of
loving" (Williams, *Modern Tragedy*, 106, 108). What Williams describes is the typical content of the *Enquirer*: "Rock Hudson's Sinister
Secret: He Hid AIDS for a Year" (*Enquirer Special: Scandals of the
Rich and Famous*, fall 1990, 4); "Dolly's Jealous Hubby Explodes.
Marriage crisis as he demands: Stop fooling around; I'm tired of sleeping alone" (*Enquirer*, September 18, 1990, cover). In private tragedy,
Williams writes, isolated characters collide with each other in "brief
experiences of physical union" that threaten "the isolation which is
all that is known of individuality" (112). It should not be surprising,

then, that the *Enquirer* shares so much of Strindberg's vision, could even have been written by Strindberg. One issue of the *Enquirer* has articles on the rise of the poor and hard-working, the fall of the rich and famous, the problem of children facing their parents' infidelities, the joy of having affairs, the trauma of ending affairs, the impossibility of heroism, the need to protect oneself, and the general vulnerability of women. These constitute a nearly complete catalogue of the themes of Strindberg's *Miss Julie*. Raymond Williams cites the plays of Tennessee Williams as the best example of this kind of tragedy, and here, too, the similarities to the tabloids are apparent: "His characters are isolated beings who desire and eat and fight alone, who struggle feverishly with the primary and related energies of love and death" (119). The *Enquirer* puts it this way: "Rape and Murder Drove Connie Francis to Psycho Ward Hell" (*Enquirer Special: Scandals of the Rich and Famous*, fall 1990, 41).

Put off by sensational content and by the apparent pandering to the worst tastes of a mass audience, literary critics have had little to say about supermarket tabloids such as *The National Enquirer*. Yet it is literary critics, above all others, who have the tools necessary to read the meanings of such literary texts, who can identify the literary characteristics of the tabloids, place them as genre, and interpret them accordingly. This new tragedy may be a fragmented form, but it is no less interesting than forms that have come before. It is also, in some respects at least, quite similar to the forms that have come before. In *Tragedy and After: Euripides, Shakespeare, Goethe*, Ekbert Faas uses the terms *anti-tragedy* and *post-tragedy* for the theater of the absurd and for Shakespearean romance, respectively, and the characteristics he enumerates for these forms come very close to describing the major characteristics of supermarket tabloids as well. Instead of the beginning, middle, and end of traditional drama, Shakespeare and Beckett "show that things are basically unpredictable, repetitive, unfathomable—in short, independent of human meaning. Their forms abound with loose ends, digressions, broken-backed structures, and fake solutions" (7). What Shakespeare and Beckett communicate to the audience that gathers in the theater, the *Enquirer* and *People* communicate to an audience that stands in supermarket checkout lines.

More than a generation ago Robert Warshow argued in a groundbreaking essay that the gangster film of the 1930s was tragedy. There was a rise and a fall in the life of the gangster, what we could identify as its tragic structure, and "the gangster is doomed because he is under the obligation to succeed, not because the means he employs are unlawful," what Warshow identified as "our intolerable dilemma: that failure is a kind of death and success is evil and dangerous, is—ultimately—impossible" ("Gangster as Tragic Hero," 133). Preoccupied as they are with success and failure, supermarket tabloids and slick gossip magazines show us both steady upward progress and precipitate falls, show us, above all else, that success is temporary and impossible to sustain or that it comes at great personal cost. Warshow wrote that the gangster "speaks for us, expressing that part of the American psyche which rejects the qualities and the demands of modern life, which rejects 'Americanism' itself" (130). The tabloids present a slightly different version of this story, for their characters accept and embrace the qualities and demands of modern life, are rewarded generously for it, and then, typically, lose it all. Sometimes they gain it right back. One of the great psychological appeals of consumer society is the belief that with success comes wealth, and with wealth comes happiness. The *Enquirer* and the other tabloids show that the belief is mistaken, that the great promises of the economic system are lies, at least for some people. They are, then, properly considered, the great tragedies of consumer society.

The great tragedies of the past identified public opinion, gossip, and scandal-mongering as the great evil, the precipitating cause of the fall of the protagonists. In the *Hippolytus* Phaedra reveals the secret of her passion for Hippolytus to her nurse, who functions within the tale as a sort of *Enquirer* reporter. The nurse publishes the information and Phaedra is destroyed. Inquiring minds wanted to know. In *Miss Julie* it is fear of public humiliation that drives Julie to suicide. In *Ghosts* Parson Manders sets up the tragic situation out of his fear of offending public opinion. The great tragedies of our own time, on the other hand, take up the point of view of public opinion. We have moved full circle, from the tragedy that sympathizes with the individual in his struggle with society, to the tragedy that sympathizes with society. It is this, finally, that a close reading of the *Enquirer* and *People* leads us to understand.

PART 2

Values

Texts are places where power and weakness become visible
and discussable, where learning and ignorance manifest
themselves, where the structures that enable and constrain
our thoughts and actions become palpable.

Robert Scholes, *Textual Power* (1985)

CHAPTER 7

Advertising and Utopia

The most powerful story we know is told to us by advertisers, a fiction about beautiful people who live for their own pleasure in a just and happy society. Poverty, suffering, and hate do not exist, and although few people work, there are more than enough goods and services to satisfy their needs—everything from breakfast cereals and deodorant to long-distance telephone service and beer. People consume these products constantly and compulsively, and if they sometimes also swallow pain killers and digestive aids along the way, this seems a small price to pay for so much good fortune. They are self-centered, indulgent, and materialistic beyond measure, and yet the world in which they live seems better than ours, as if their selfishness has turned out to be a kind of virtue. "Self denial? Me? Ha!" an elegantly sensual young woman exclaims in an advertisement for Breyer's Natural Light Ice Cream, articulating the most dearly held belief of the community. However much she eats she will never gain any weight, never look any less beautiful, and, in fact, because eating throws her into sensual rapture—she is photographed in soft focus in a close-up with her eyes closed, erotically caressing a spoon—the more she eats the more beautiful she will be. "It just doesn't get any better than this," generations of Old Milwaukee beer drinkers have told us, convinced they are speaking the truth. It's a fantasy, of course, a complex and elaborate fiction that has become the background against which we live and measure our lives.

The story is powerful not only because so much money is spent in selling it to us in so many different forms, but also because it is a contemporary version of two of the oldest and most important stories of our culture brilliantly brought together, the tale of the golden age and the story of utopia. Individuals live for their own pleasure in the fictions that describe a golden age, a story form we can trace back as far as ancient Sumeria and find fully developed in ancient Greek and Hebrew literature, in Homer's description of Calypso's grotto in *The Odyssey*, in the poetry of Hesiod and Pindar, and in the Old Testament story of the Garden of Eden. Individuals live in a society without poverty, injustice, or hate in the utopia, a story that derives from the tale of the golden age and begins with Plato's *Republic*, developing later with St. Augustine's description of the New Jerusalem (Christianity's defining utopia) and with Sir Thomas More's *Utopia*, which gives the genre its name and its standard form during the Renaissance. These are fundamental texts of Western culture, stories about what constitutes the good life and the good society that initiate a tradition of storytelling within which advertising should be read and understood. The naked men and women who embrace in artistic combinations under the influence of Calvin Klein perfumes, the health-conscious women who exercise hard in their Reebok shoes, and the wise old gardener who uses Miracle Gro plant food to produce miraculous tomatoes all belong to the traditions of the golden age and utopia as they have been adapted to the needs of consumer society.

Because utopias are visions of a better world they have frequently been seen as protests against the dominant ideology of their own times. Thus the terms *ideology* and *utopia* are often paired by critics, *ideology* meaning the prevailing values and beliefs of a society, especially as they support the classes or groups of people in power, *utopia* connoting a protest against that ideology. More's *Utopia*, an attack on a society based on private property and a description of an alternative society based on virtue, set up such a pattern in the other utopias created on its model. Advertising, however, cleverly unites ideology and utopia, destroying this traditional opposition and giving us the vision of a better world as imagined by private property. Most utopias have been created in the past by poets and philosophers who believed that through reason humankind could create a better world, but few authors in the twentieth century have been so confident. In their place, American advertising agencies have appropriated the story form, not because top executives have been busy reading Plato, St. Augustine, or More, but because advertisers have learned how to manipulate our emotional needs and we have turned out to be particularly vulnerable to stories that equate pleasure with justice. There is nothing particularly philosophical or theological about this, only the commercial impulse to sell us goods and services, many of which we really don't need. All those little stories about how the big oil companies care about nature, the big telephone companies care about families, and the big athletic shoe companies care about our physical and spiritual well-being add up to a seductive apotheosis of capitalism as virtue.

In the tales of the golden age you do what you want; in utopia you do what you should; and in the advertising story, want and should are exactly the same. It is no wonder, then, that by uniting the tale of the golden age with utopia advertising has created an overwhelmingly powerful story form. With respect to its attitude toward pleasure, its most obvious characteristic, advertising most closely resembles the tales of the golden age. Chewing gum and Jell-O grow on trees, bottles of Grand Marnier are trees, Mazola corn oil pours directly from stalk to bottle, and cans of Lone Star beer rise magically from the earth. "He's not married or anything. *And* he drinks Johnnie Walker Red," two women tell each other somewhat drunkenly as they sit in a bar, leaning on each other for support and laughing at their immense good fortune. He has, after all, the two characteristics they are looking for in a man. "Good taste is always an asset," the line at the bottom of the advertisement explains. With respect to its structure and organization, advertising most closely resembles the tradition of utopia, a society with its own set of customs and institutions. Happy Saturn workers produce automobiles in spotlessly clean factories, the U.S. Postal Service always delivers the mail on time, and everybody is in good hands with the Allstate Insurance Company. But the similarities between advertising and utopia and the golden age go far deeper: the generalized character of the consumers who appear in ads, their lack of diversity, the stress on consumption rather than production, and the nearly total absence of conflict are all traditional features either of the golden age or of utopia. Not everything is the same in advertising, however. Personal freedom is important in the tales of the golden age and social justice in utopia; the freedom at issue in advertising is no real freedom at all, and social justice is achieved only by making the poor disappear altogether. Everyone can wander off in a Winnebago or drive a Toyota 4×4 up a pile of rocks, but nobody is really free and nobody can truly wander. No one is homeless, or seriously ill, or discriminated against, and the only real problem ever faced by African Americans is diarrhea. They are too busy and much too happy playing basketball, which is pretty much their only occupation aside from a little football and baseball.

More's *Utopia*

There are few better guides to the nature of contemporary American advertising than More's *Utopia*, not because they differ on some fundamental principles or agree on others, but because almost everything that is an explicit concern in *Utopia* is implicit in what I will call adtopia. More makes clear what advertisers do their best to obscure: that pleasure comes at a price for all of us, and that we had better pick our pleasures wisely; that there are important ethical issues involved in every choice that we make, no matter how small; that what we are taught to value as individuals affects the well-being of our entire society; and that everything finally fits together—the freedom we value, the clothes we buy, the religion we practice, the possessions we acquire, the sex we experience, the privacy we allow. In many of its most fundamental principles, certainly, *Utopia* is very different from adtopia. More's vision of the best of all possible worlds, first published in 1516, is of a society based on virtue, work, study, and monogamy, where idleness, luxury, sexual promiscuity, and private property are crimes against the state. Adtopia, created by American advertising agencies in the second half of the twentieth century, is the exact opposite kind of society, one that might accurately be described as More's worst nightmare, a society based on idleness, luxury, sexual indulgence, and material wealth. Does that matter? It depends on the power and influence we are willing to attribute to utopian visions. If the critics are right who argue that we reveal our deepest aspirations in utopia, then it may matter a good deal that it is adtopia we learn about in hundreds of little fragments every day of our lives, rather than the lessons of *Utopia*. Idleness and gambling are not allowed in More's Utopia, where individuals use their free time to cultivate their minds; by contrast, idleness and gambling are desirable activities in adtopia, where individuals use their free time to consume things. This is a fundamental difference in values. The wise men in Utopia are its priests, who lead their followers in a celebration of spiritual truth and the nature of faith, whereas the wise men and women in adtopia are its master consumers, who lead their followers in a celebration of material truth and the nature of coffeemakers. There are some spiritual men and women in adtopia, to be sure, but these are for the most part solitary runners, decked out in their Reeboks and Nikes, who find themselves near the tops of mountains.

"I don't see how you can ever get any real justice or prosperity, so long as there's private property, and everything's judged in terms of money," More's guide to Utopia, Raphael Hythloday, tells him, "unless you consider it just for the worst sort of people to have the best living conditions, or unless you're prepared to call a country prosperous, in which all the wealth is owned by a tiny minority—who aren't entirely happy even so, while everyone else is simply miserable" (*Utopia*, 65). In adtopia there is justice and prosperity precisely because of private property, and although there are different living conditions— the guys at the bar arguing about whether Miller Lite is less filling or has great taste are not in the same class as the elderly gentlemen driving around in their Rolls Royces trying to score some Grey Poupon— the inequities of wealth are not as great as those described by Hythloday. No one is poor and no one has to go without anything, except perhaps for health insurance in that little part of the story written by politicians pushing for universal health care. The issue of misery is a little more complicated, however, and we will come back to it later. But on the surface, at least, no one suffers in adtopia.

Money and the things it can buy are the greatest evil in Utopia, the greatest good in adtopia. The pleasures of the mind are most valuable in Utopia, the pleasures of the body dangerous distractions. Adtopia inverts this as well. The pleasures of the body are the most cherished in adtopia; the pleasures of the mind are few and far between and limited exclusively to young children enthralled by the latest computer and video technology. We have, to paraphrase the Virginia Slims advertising campaign, come a long way, baby, from the deeply moral and fundamentally Christian world conceived by More, a man who urged his readers to love learning, worship God, and control desire. Jewelry is given to small children as a plaything in Utopia, because gems are shiny and appeal to childish sensibilities but are otherwise useless, and criminals are forced to wear gold chains, but no adult Utopian values such materials. In adtopia, on the other hand, women are constantly shown fondling themselves while holding jewelry and wearing gold. Elizabeth Taylor has made an entire career of it. You must never want too much for yourself in Utopia, but you can never have too much for yourself in adtopia.

Like other thinkers of his time, More was convinced that the "beastly root of all evils" was pride. "For pride's criterion of prosperity is not what you've got yourself, but what other people haven't got. Pride would refuse to set foot in paradise, if she thought there'd be no under-privileged classes there to gloat over and order about—nobody whose misery could serve as a foil for her own happiness" (131). Pride is the root of all good in adtopia, the reason middle-aged men drive Buicks, women of all ages carry Gucci bags, and teenage boys play basketball in sneakers filled with bells and whistles. They are responsible for driving the economy. Pride does set foot in the paradise that is adtopia, even though there are no underprivileged classes to gloat over and order about, for anyone can get the car, the bag, or the shoes. Misery is no longer the necessary foil for happiness, only the temporary condition of a consumer who has made a wrong product choice.

In order to end pride More decided to eliminate individuality. No one is a strong individual in Utopia since it is the good of the community that matters. Everyone wears identical clothing, lives in shared houses, eats in communal dining halls, and has absolutely no privacy. In adtopia, on the other hand, it is the individual that counts, not the larger community, about which very few people or institutions care at all, save perhaps for the telephone company. Clothing is a major obsession for adtopians, who express their individuality through dress, housing, food, and their use of privacy. Everyone watches everyone else in Utopia so that no one has the opportunity to be different, to go off alone, to avoid work, to be free. Everyone watches everyone else in adtopia because everyone is constantly on the make, flirting, admiring, seducing, playing, being free. What comes along with this level of individuality and concern for self is exactly the kind of behavior More wished to eliminate: "To assume he is uncaring or aloof is to misread him," an advertisement for Egoïste Cologne by Chanel explains. "He walks on the positive side of that fine line separating arrogance from an awareness of self-worth." In adtopia a cold, unfeeling man like this turns out to be a really great guy.

But if adtopia is in these respects a mirror image of Utopia, it shares
a number of other characteristics with More's fiction, including a sense
of the comic, an interest in the power relations between people, and
a hierarchy of pleasure. *Utopia* is not altogether serious, and its various pronouncements on the nature of society are lightened by the
comic improbabilities of the place and the individuals involved with
it. There are times when it simply seems like one big joke. Similarly,
adtopia is not altogether serious, what with its pink Energizer bunny
who keeps going and going through clever parodies of advertisements,
crones asking, "Where's the beef?" and Big Star hamburgers dripping
special sauce. There are times when it, too, simply seems like one big
joke. Ultimately, however, the jokes reinforce the basic (and serious)
message. Utopians command slaves and husbands command wives in
a series of fixed and absolute power relations between human beings.
Adtopians live in a society where power relations shift constantly, and
many individual ads show the struggle between men and women, husbands and wives. Although there are no slaves, much of the dirty work
in adtopia is done by women.

Utopians believe that "human happiness consists largely or wholly
in pleasure" (91) and that "the enjoyment of life—that is, pleasure"
is "the natural object of all human efforts" (92). So do adtopians.
Considerably more advanced in their understanding of pleasure than
most adtopians, however, the Utopians discriminate between pleasures that are natural and unnatural, major and minor, healthful and
harmful. They think about consequences, meaning, and significance.
Sexual intercourse is a real pleasure in Utopia, for example, but it is
the most basic physical kind—More groups it with rubbing, scratch-
ing, and excreting. Much more important are the physical pleasures
that come from having a healthy, well-functioning body, the "natural
gifts such as beauty, strength, and agility" (98), and greater yet are
the mental pleasures that come from a contemplation of ideas. This is
a Platonic hierarchy, a progression from body to spirit that parallels
the movement from youth to maturity. A similar if somewhat more
limited hierarchy exists in adtopia, where youthful preoccupations
with sex and beauty sometimes give way to more mature concerns
with strength, health, and agility, but it is sex that gets the most
attention. The Utopians restrict sexual activity to marriage because
they understand that there would be no reason for them to marry

otherwise. The adtopians do not, and often find no reason to marry at all. "I got Midas-ized in Waco, Texas," one satisfied adtopian drawls. "You never saw a muffler so big."

Adtopia

American advertising, dominated by its utopian elements, presents a vision of pleasure, desire, and limited freedom. What we find when we examine it as a culture is as strange and wondrous as anything Hythloday found in Utopia. A young woman in a bikini floats in a swimming pool while next to her a bottle of Pernod emerges from the water held by a male hand. The liquid from the bottle spouts upward and then arches over into a glass that rests on her stomach. The Pernod does not impregnate the woman in the traditional way; it aims for her stomach, a more important erogenous zone in adtopia (along with the mouth and armpit). We do not have a word to define this activity, although both Freud and Marx would call it a fetish—for Freud, an example of misplaced sexual energy, for Marx, an example of an object relationship replacing a human relationship. Combining *sodomy* (as a general term for sexual relations between human and nonhuman) with *commodity*, we devise *commodomy* and coin a name for the most peculiar activity in adtopia. Such an activity may be easy to denounce as perverse, but it is only part of the larger concern for self in adtopia.

Another sight Hythloday would have been amazed at is the reversal of moral order in adtopia. The seven deadly sins of More's church have become the cardinal virtues of adtopia. Gluttony, lust, sloth, pride, covetousness, envy, and anger all show up in advertisements, either as ordinary, acceptable behaviors or as desirable ones. Fat, flabby men luxuriate on cruise ships and sigh with pleasure over the food. Other consumers, the habitual overeaters, overdrinkers, and overindulgers, dismiss the minor discomforts with stomach tablets. Women envy each other's coffee, hair dye, and coconut cake. Men lust after women. Together they covet all manner of products. And beyond that, they are intensely vain. "I love a mysterious woman who exudes vanity," a hairstylist explains. "I think everyone should be mysterious and vain." One of the vainest is a woman in an advertisement for swimming pools. Dressed in a polo outfit and standing by her grand piano, she boasts: "Philip is profoundly aware of my innate need to satisfy me, me, me. So is Mission Pools." Medieval hell has become our modern utopia. In another ad, showing two men in fancy dress clothes, the text reads, "The Meek Shall Inherit Very Little."

Adtopians belong to one of two social classes, the very rich or the middle class. The rich live in the lush green countryside of adtopia, the middle class in the large suburban developments that cover the remaining land. The two groups live very different kinds of lives. The very rich live in large mansions, ride horses, and in general behave like eighteenth-century aristocrats. Some cultivate the style of the landed gentry in England before the industrial revolution (Scotch advertisements), others the style of the Russian nobility before the 1917 revolution (vodka advertisements). In either mode they live only to indulge themselves, lavishing attention and wealth on the best clothes, rugs, cosmetics, and liquor. In Karl Mannheim's sense (*Ideology and Utopia*), we have the utopia of the conservative ideal, for almost no signs of technology or practicality intrude into this pastoral, almost medieval romance. The middle class, on the other hand, lives close to technology, in smaller, more modest homes, which they are constantly cleaning. They are the great homemakers of adtopia, who must pay attention to the more practical aspects of existence, to discovering which supermarket has the lowest prices overall and which toothpaste will best prevent tooth decay.

Within this social structure, human growth and development take place, particularly among the middle class, who exist in the present and who pass through distinct stages of individual life. Following a blissful childhood of playing, eating candy and sugar-coated cereal, and making occasional visits to the dentist, the good middle-class individual advances through three stages of life: early adulthood, late adulthood, and sagehood. During early adulthood, which lasts until age thirty or marriage, whichever comes first, men are strong, forceful, and handsome, women submissive and beautiful. Like the very rich, these people live only for pleasure, boasting that they smoke cigarettes for taste, and staring provocatively from advertisements for liquor, fast cars, and toiletries. The man seduces; the woman is seduced— until marriage. Then they appear in ads for medicines, laundry soaps, and breakfast cereals. The men seem preoccupied, no longer sure they smoke for taste. As they begin worrying about the tar count, they experience a sudden loss of power and control, falling back on their wives, who must help them remember to take vitamins or buy the best items at the supermarket. During this troubled period of mature adulthood women come into their own, becoming strong as men become weak. As smart and knowledgeable shoppers, these are the people to whom the admen speak directly. In these close and frequent contacts, they begin to pick up the characteristics of admen—they start enjoying power over others beyond their immediate family, and as they grow progressively older and wiser, they influence more and more of their neighbors. Finally, at the end of mature adulthood, a very few of these wise shoppers (including an occasional male) enter sagehood. They stand before us and urge us to eat our oatmeal with an authority we respect. So valued are these people that they are the only ones in adtopia who have names—individuals like those we knew a generation ago as Mrs. Olsen, Mr. Whipple, Aunt Blue Bell, and Madge. Nevertheless, some of these characters suggest that sagacity fades into senility, the very last bit of wisdom the character retains being attachment to product. What these senile sages have, beyond wisdom about products, is a Benthamite balance between pleasure-seeking and pain-avoiding, the quality that makes them most endearing and useful to the entire population. Madge has a product that allows women to wash dishes and give themselves a beauty treatment at the same time.

Adtopians mature in a peculiarly limited fashion, from the pleasure-seeking of immediate gratification through the pain-avoiding of delayed gratification, finally arriving at the wisdom of combining both. The first two stages follow the broad outlines of Freud's pleasure principle and reality principle. To that extent the development of adtopians appears perfectly normal, yet their lives under the reality principle cannot grow beyond adtopian reality. All three stages, in fact, follow a much more specific and revealing pattern, that of hedonism. Herbert Marcuse distinguishes three stages of hedonism in classical philosophy: (1) pleasure-seeking; (2) pain-avoiding; and (3) Epicurean, or the balancing of pleasure and pain. The pleasure seekers "avoid interpersonal relations, for these are based on understanding and knowledge, which they discover to be contrary to happiness." The pain avoiders fear "the insecurity and badness of the conditions of life, the invincible limitation of enjoyment." Ultimately, Marcuse argues, this gives way to perfect Epicureanism, where the exercise of reason itself becomes a pleasure and the tranquility of the sage becomes the final goal ("On Hedonism," 165–72).

In Marcuse's description we begin to see what the adtopians have traded for their life of econo-eroticism. Recapitulating the history of classical hedonism, the adtopians relieve their ancient problems: the careful avoidance of interpersonal relations, the fear of knowledge, and the loss of meaningful understanding or control over their lives. However much they may grow beyond simple pleasure-seeking, they never grow beyond hedonism. They suffer from the illnesses Kierkegaard catalogues as the aesthetic—malaise, anxiety, and boredom— in spite of the pleasures they experience. A young, expensively dressed woman lies on a chaise, looking off to one side vacantly, with a Waterman pen in her hand. "I gave up cigarettes. I gave up expresso. I gave up the Count (that naughty man). And his little house in Cap Ferrat. The Waterman, however is not negotiable. I must have something thrilling with which to record my boredom." These pleasure seekers fail precisely where Kierkegaard said they would—meaningful decision making—and in the existential sense they do not exist. Their pathologies turn up in the ailments from which they suffer—constipation, headache, insomnia, and hemorrhoids, all of which they treat but never cure. Incredibly restless, they move from brand to brand, always hoping the next will satisfy their needs. When they do have opportunities to make choices, their decisions are rendered nearly meaningless by the nature of the choice. A businessman waits to catch his evening commuter train. "The 5:42 or not the 5:42? That is the question," he thinks to himself. "Or is it nobler to catch the 6:11? Forsooth McGinty," the man cries, loosening his collar and speaking to an unseen bartender, "build me a Booth's martini." So trivialized is the decision when compared to Hamlet's that the consumer quite understandably turns to one of the most popular painkillers in adtopia, alcohol. But as others have noted, in utopia individuals rarely have both happiness and freedom.

Perhaps a more severe pathology than this absence of meaningful choice is the difficulty adtopians have in relating to one another. So self-centered are these people that, like the Cyrenaics, they avoid human relationships, preferring instead what adtopia offers as an improved substitute, relationships with inanimate objects. There is little mutuality in the group scenes in adtopia; what interaction does take place at picnics and parties is usually the result of consumer products that have made it easier for the consumers to get together. A naked woman lowers herself onto the back of a nearly naked man, who is wearing sun glasses. She says, "Only if you promise to keep those sunglasses on." Sex is fine, but intimacy is another matter altogether. Given the choice between a relationship with another person or a relationship with a product, many adtopians prefer the latter. A remarkable advertisement for a Sony personal television shows a middle-aged couple in bed. The headline explains, "There comes a time in everyone's life when you just want to be alone with the person you love." The husband and wife both have their own personal Sony TVs in bed with them. They are watching their TVs intently; they have turned their backs on each other. These people are committing a simple act of commodomy. An elegantly dressed woman closes her eyes and leans over to kiss a statue. "La passione di Roma," the text explains, in an advertisement for Fendi perfume.

For these people the commodomy is entirely pleasurable; but for others in adtopia, even the man-object relationship has moved out of their control. So weakened and disoriented do some consumers become that products control them. This is especially clear in the development of products that talk to consumers and direct their behavior. In most advertising, the human being encounters the product through the mediation of another customer or an adman—but occasionally, these product representatives have taken nonhuman form, such as the Trix rabbit and the Pillsbury Doughboy. There are also direct encounters between product and consumer. In the now-classic television series for Parkay margarine, human and product turn the consumption relationship into what Martin Buber would classify as "I-Thou." In a typical version of this ad, a middle-aged man has come into his kitchen late at night for a snack. He takes food carefully from the refrigerator to avoid waking his wife, who can be seen vaguely in the background. Suddenly a voice breaks the silence—"Butter." It is a rich, somewhat silly-sounding voice, and it comes from the box of margarine. Although the man is surprised and worried that the box will wake his wife, he is soon drawn into the argument with the margarine. The margarine stubbornly insists that it is butter and the man just as stubbornly insists that it is margarine. Finally he tastes the product and decides it must be butter. "Butter," he admits sheepishly, but the margarine responds, slowly, tauntingly, "Parkay." In the next room, his wife mutters fitfully in her sleep. The encounter is over. This relationship goes far beyond commodomy, for with language comes control. The Parkay has a limited vocabulary—only natural for a first tentative encounter between animate and inanimate world—but the margarine is not to be taken lightly, for it wins the interaction with the human. It successfully tricks a man of seemingly normal intelligence, and in so doing it also reveals its own margarinelike personality as trickster.

There are important trade-offs in More's *Utopia* as well. There is no privacy, individuality, or free travel, no wealth, ostentation, or sexual freedom, and everyone's clothes are exactly the same. What the citizens of Utopia get in return is a world with social justice and without suffering. In adtopia there is privacy, individuality, free travel, lots of different clothes, great wealth, ostentation, and sexual freedom. What the citizens of adtopia get in return is a world where decision making is meaningless, where people actually prefer to be with their things rather than with other people, and where these things have come to hold power over them. Who gets the better deal? The drawbacks of what advertising promises are not hidden from our view, only lost in the fragmentary nature of individual ads, and any covenant we enter into with it comes with the opportunity to know its true nature.

The "most important changes in the intellectual structure of the modern world are to be understood in the light of the transformation of the utopian element," Karl Mannheim writes in *Ideology and Utopia*. He distinguishes four distinct stages of utopia in Western history, each succeeding the other in dialectical fashion: a theology based on ecstatic mysticism; a liberal humanitarianism based on reason and concerned with the ideal; a conservative counterutopia based on the status quo and concerned with the material; and finally the socialist-communist utopia, which combines the freedom of earlier forms with the materialism of the conservative counterutopia. This dialectic ends for Mannheim with the socialist-communist utopia, but if we accept his process without accepting his stopping point (*Ideology and Utopia* appeared in 1936), then we can see adtopia as a fifth stage, an overwhelmingly conservative response to the socialist-communist utopia that contains elements of all earlier utopian forms. The advertising text represents the last of a series of transformations of utopian thought from the medieval concept of heaven to the nineteenth-century concept of a classless society. Advertising does not deny the charges made by Marx and his followers about capitalism; rather, it admits them and makes them central to its vision of the good life. Reification and the fetishism of commodities, denounced by Marxists, become the glory of the capitalist adtopia. "Reification,"

Georg Lukacs writes in *History and Class Consciousness* (1923), "requires that a society should learn to satisfy all its needs in terms of commodity exchange" (91). In ways that neither Marx nor Lukacs could foresee, however, advertising has turned these dismal characteristics into romance.

CHAPTER 8

The Shopping Mall and the Formal Garden

The contemporary shopping mall is the great formal garden of American culture, a commercial space that shares fundamental characteristics with many of the great garden styles of Western history. Set apart from the rest of the world as a place of earthly delight like the medieval walled garden; filled with fountains, statuary, and ingeniously devised machinery like the Italian Renaissance garden; designed on grandiose and symmetrical principles like the seventeenth-century French garden; made up of the fragments of cultural and architectural history like the eighteenth-century irregular English garden; and set aside for the public like the nineteenth-century American park, the mall is the next phase of this garden history, a synthesis of all these styles that have come before. But it is now joined with the shopping street, or at least a sanitized and standardized version of one, something never before allowed within the garden. In this latest version of the earthly paradise, people live on the goods of the consumer economy peacefully, pleasurably, and even with sophisticated complexity, for although their pleasure comes from buying and everything is set up to facilitate that pleasure, the garden itself is no simple place. Nordstrom has come to Eden. There were dangers and temptations in the very first garden, of course, and the delights dangled before us have been equally powerful. We have moved from the knowledge of good and evil to the joys of shopping.

Visitors learn the meanings of consumer society at the mall, not only in the choices they make in their purchases but also in the symbol systems they walk through, just as visitors to those earlier gardens were invited to learn about the meanings of their own times from the pastoral adventures presented to them. Like the formal garden, the shopping mall is a construct of promenades, walls, vistas, mounts, labyrinths, fountains, statues, archways, trees, grottoes, theaters, flowering plants and shrubs, trellises, and assorted reproductions from architectural history, all artfully arranged. Some of these features, such as the mount, have undergone technological or economic modification. The mount—the manmade earthworks designed to present a vista of the garden to the visitor and typically reached by path or staircase—was a standard part of garden design from the Middle Ages to the eighteenth century. This has been replaced by the escalator, which rises at key points in the enclosed central parts of the mall, where it presents a similar vista of the space to the visitor, who is now lifted dramatically from the floor below by unseen forces without any effort on his or her part. And this, in its turn, is only a modification of a standard feature from Italian Renaissance gardens, the elaborate hydraulic machinery or automata that engineers had devised to move statues about in striking dramatic tableaux. Now in the mall it is the visitors who are moved about by the escalators, becoming themselves the actors in a tableau we might title "modern shopping." Combining the mount with the automata, the mall then encloses this machinery in two or three stories of space, topped with skylights. The result is something like Houston's Galleria Mall, a massive, three-story, enclosed mall topped with skylights. This, in turn, is an updated version of Henry VIII's great garden at Hampton Court, where a mount was topped by a three-story glass arbor surrounded by figures of the king's beasts and a royal crown. We have dispensed with the beasts and crown; joggers now run on the roof of the Galleria. But the mount in the king's garden allowed the visitor to look both inside and outside of his garden; the escalator within the enclosed mall of the Galleria, by contrast, only allows the visitor to look at the inside space.

Similarly, the labyrinth—the maze of pathways or hedges that confounded the visitor's attempts to find a easy way out and was a favorite device of Renaissance gardens—is now the cleverly laid out pattern of aisles within department stores, which can be designed to discourage the visitor's easy exit. Shoppers simply cannot find a way out. A decade ago Bloomingdale's in the Willow Grove Mall in suburban Philadelphia received so many complaints from irate shoppers lost in its mazes that finally small, discreet exit signs were posted. What might have originated in the mazes of the early Christian Church, which penitents traveled on their knees while praying at particular points, was first moved outside into the garden, where it was secularized, and has now become thoroughly commodified, a journey in which purchases have replaced prayers. Buy enough and we will let you out.

Played against the maze and labyrinth in the Renaissance garden were the axial and radial avenues that began as extensions of the hallways of the palace and ended in suitably grand natural vistas. Played against the department store maze in the mall are the axial and radial avenues that begin as extensions of hallways of one anchor department store and end in the grand vistas of the entrances to other anchor department stores.

The kitchen garden, that area of the formal garden closest to the house and set aside for the production of food, has become the food court, that area of the mall set aside for the consumption of food. The statues—the assorted imitations of Greek and Roman models, portraits of contemporary royalty, or stylized representations of the ancient virtues—have become mannequins decked out in fashionable clothing, the generalized imitations of consumers in their most beautiful, heroic, and changeable poses, portraits of contemporary anonymous life that we should see as stylized representations of the modern virtues: pose, flexibility, nubility, interchangeability, emotional absence. The generalized faces on the statues are now the empty faces of the mannequins. And the various architectural antiquities that became a feature of eighteenth-century English irregular gardens—the miscellaneous copies of Greek temples, Gothic ruins, Japanese pagodas, Roman triumphal arches, and Italian grottoes—are now represented not so much by the miscellaneous architectural reproductions that appear seasonally in the mall, as in the Easter Bunny's cottage or Santa's Workshop, but much more profoundly by many of the stores themselves, which present idealized versions of architectural and cultural history to the consumer: the Victorian lingerie shop, the high modernist fur salon, the nineteenth-century Western goods store, the Mexican restaurant, the country store designed as a red barn, the dark bar designed as a grotto. Also present in smaller details—in the grand

staircase, the wall of mirrors, the plush carpeting, the man playing the
white grand piano—are echoes of the 1930s movie set; in the merry-
go-round, the popcorn cart, and the clown with balloons, the echoes
of funland. The eighteenth-century garden included such historical reproductions in an effort to make sense of its past and to accommodate
its cultural inheritances to new situations. One can say the same about
the mall's inclusion of historical recollections. If we judge this to be
playful and parodic, then we can also call the space postmodern, but
if it is only a nostalgic recovery of history, we cannot. This can be a
tricky thing. The mall's appropriation of history into idealized spaces
of consumption can be nostalgia or parody, or both at the same time.

The Stanford Shopping Center near Palo Alto presents such a parodic and nostalgic bricolage of cultural and architectural history:
Crabtree and Evelyn with its images of eighteenth-century life; Laura
Ashley with its images of Romantic and early Victorian life; Victoria's
Secret, the late Victorian whorehouse with overtones of French fashion; Banana Republic, the late Victorian colonial outfitter; the Disney
Store with its images of 1940s art; and The Nature Company, closest
to the sixteenth century and the rise of science in its stock of simple
instruments and decor of simple observations of nature. One walks
through the images of history just as one did in the formal garden, but
now they can be appropriated through the act of consuming. One buys
images but learns "history." It is a clean, neat, middle-class version of
history without the homeless of a downtown big city, and thus a re-
treat from the frenzy of urban life and of contemporary history, which
is exactly what the formal garden was also designed to be. To one side
is an alley devoted to food: a lavishly idealized greengrocer, a pseudo-
Italian coffee bar, and Max's Opera Cafe, a reproduction of a grand
nineteenth-century cafe in Vienna—but what one finds when one wanders inside is not real or ersatz Vienna, but a glorified Jewish deli. Here
the history of central Europe is rewritten as it might have been.

In one Renaissance garden a grotto dedicated to Venus and voluptuous pleasure was juxtaposed with one dedicated to Diana and virtuous pleasure. In another a Temple of Ancient Virtue was contrasted
with one representing Modern Virtue. In a similar manner the visitor
to the modern garden at Stanford is presented with choices between
Victoria's Secret, the shop of voluptuous pleasure, and Westminister
Lace, the shop of virtuous pleasure and chastity, but he or she does
not have to choose between the Temple of Modern Virtue, the modern

shopping center itself, or the Temple of Ancient Virtue, the remnants of the gardens of the past, because the mall artfully combines both.

We are almost at an end of our catalogue of garden elements. In fact, the only standard feature of garden design not present in the modern mall, either in original or in modified form, is the hermitage ruin, a favorite eighteenth-century architectural device designed to allow the visitor to pretend to be a hermit, to be alone and to meditate. There are only two places where a visitor can be alone in the mall: in the lavatories and in the clothing store changing room, but even there one can find surveillance cameras. Meditation and isolation are not virtues encouraged by the modern garden because, interestingly enough, given the opportunity, too many consumers will not meditate there at all, but try to steal whatever they can.

The shopping mall is, of course, quite an imperfect paradise, but the fault does not lie so much with the garden as with the shopping street it has come to assimilate. It is true that there are very few trees in these postmodern gardens, and those that do appear are typically confined in antipastoral concrete planters, but such subordination of nature has occurred before in garden history. Plants were incidental to the Renaissance garden, where visitors instead were expected to direct their attention to the grottoes, fountains, and various mechanical automata.

By bringing the mundane world of commerce into the garden, along with its attendant ills, the mall appears to be inverting the fundamental purposes of many of those earlier gardens as places of repose and contemplation, of escape from the mundane world. Conspicuous consumption has replaced quiet repose. But many of the great styles of garden history have been practical, if not precisely in this way, for example, the *ferme ornée* or eighteenth-century ornamented working farm with its fields, kitchen gardens, orchards, and pastures placed beside the more decorative and formal elements of the garden. These were gardens that had their practical commercial aspects. But although the mall is a far more commercial place than the practical garden, the shift has not so much destroyed the garden—for most of history a space set aside for the rich—as adapted it to new social and economic realities, and it thus can be seen as the appropriate garden for a consumer-oriented culture. In the formal gardens of the past, where nature was rearranged to fit the aesthetic taste of the period, one walked through the landscape contemplating the vistas and approaching the beautiful. In the shopping mall, where nature is similarly rearranged to fit the commercial needs of the period, one walks through the landscape, now contemplating not the vistas of nature, which have been completely blocked out, but rather the vistas presented by the entrances to the anchor department stores, and now approaching not the beautiful but rather the commodities by means of which one can become beautiful. These are practical times. The aristocrat who walked down the path of the garden admired the flowers and smelled their scents; the consumer who walks down the path of the shopping mall buys the flower scents in bottles and then smells like the flower or the musk ox. The focus has shifted from the individual in reverie facing an artificial version of nature to the individual in excitement facing a garden of consumer products. In the eighteenth century the visitor to the garden was expected to feel the elevation of his or her soul. It is unlikely that the visitor to the modern mall has a comparable experience.

The Shopping Mall in the History of the Formal Garden

If the mall can be understood as a garden, against the standard elements of garden design, it can also be understood as a special moment in garden history. Garden design from the Middle Ages to the nineteenth century shows a shift from enclosed to open space, and from the seventeenth century on shows a shift from symbols of state power to symbols of individuality and liberty. Walls give way to grand natural views, and symmetrical landscapes that communicated the power of the monarch give way to irregular and "natural" spaces set aside for individual contemplation. As thinking shifts from theology to science, the garden celebrates botany rather than morality. As philosophy shifts from rationalism to empiricism, the garden changes from a place of geometrical form and shaped shrubs to a representation of a "naturally" occurring landscape. As political systems shift from regal and authoritarian to mercantile and democratic, the garden changes from an allegory of state power to an allegory of individual freedom. The enclosed, highly artificial space gradually becomes open and "natural."

But the shopping mall marks a return to enclosure, symmetry, and control, to space even more confined than the medieval walled garden and just as authoritarian as Renaissance and seventeenth-century design. The mall now encloses the sensual world once again, not simply with walls but with displays of consumer goods. Barton Creek Square, for example, built on a hill above Austin, Texas, and resembling a fortress, has one of the finest views available of the city and of the Texas hill country beyond, and is immediately adjacent to a major creek, greenbelt, and recreation area. But all the views are from the parking lots, since the mall, like so many others, is completely enclosed; the vistas inside the mall are of the grand entrances to Sears and its competitors. Where once practical buildings were blocked from sight and vistas created by the selective planting of trees and shrubs and by the creation or relocation of hillsides, as in the eighteenth-century garden, now the vista is blocked from view to produce the sight of the practical building. Where once the vista was of the grandeur of nature, it is now of the grandeur of manufactured commodities.

The medieval garden may be the most important model for the mall. Read against that garden of earthly delight and erotic dalliance, the mall is immediately very recognizable space, the place of earthly delight sealed off from the cares of the mundane world, and for many of its visitors a place of courtly dalliance and love. The teenagers who prowl our malls, preening and flirting, are making an essentially medieval use of the space. In the medieval *Romance of the Rose*, for example, the poet-hero comes upon a walled garden owned by the allegorical figure of Pleasure, to which he is admitted by a sexy, young, rich, and powerful woman named Idleness. She spends her time grooming and amusing herself, of course. Hate, Treachery, Infamy, Covetousness, Greed, Envy, Sadness, Old Age, Hypocrisy, and Poverty are excluded from this garden, but within Pleasure Idleness relaxes with Youth, Beauty, Riches, Candour, Courtesy, Liberality, and the God of Love himself. The poet-hero wanders off to explore this garden, peers into the fountain of Self-Love, and sees there a perfect rose in the reflection, the symbol of his true love. When he is shot by one of Cupid's arrows, he knows he must possess this object of his passion.

With only minor modification, we have an allegorical interpretation of our shopping mall, into which the visitor is admitted by Idleness, guided by Pleasure, victimized by Self-Love, and then overtaken by Passion—not for his true love this time as much as for the endless objects of consumption that litter the garden. And although he may leave Hate, Treachery, Infamy, Sadness, Old Age, Hypocrisy, and Poverty behind, Covetousness, Greed, and Envy seem to have gained entrance to the garden, where they have joined Youth, Beauty, and Riches, while Candour, Courtesy, and Liberality appear to have disappeared altogether. We have built for ourselves, with some significant modification, the stage set upon which we act the *Romance of the Rose* every day.

But if the mall repeats the medieval garden, it is the exact inversion of the eighteenth-century garden, which was designed as a place of repose, meditation, and tranquil contemplation. The only place of tranquil contemplation in the mall would be within the occasional (and nearly always deserted) Christian Science Reading Room. The eighteenth-century garden also celebrated the pleasures of individual liberty, with vistas of open space, various places to make choices, and secluded bowers to be alone. The shopping mall celebrates the pleasures of consumption, with vistas of consumer goods, places to make economic choices, but no bowers to be alone. Introspection and reflection are discouraged, but education, nevertheless, is constantly taking place, for visitors to the mall are constantly confronted with information about the meanings of the space and their role within it.

The transition from the eighteenth-century conception of the garden as a free and open space, an aid to reflection and individuality, to the twentieth-century conception of the garden as an enclosed shopping mall is supplied by the nineteenth-century public park. In the public park the garden was opened for the first time to great masses of ordinary people, but when these benefits of freedom and liberty were extended to the riffraff the garden needed to be changed accordingly. Frederick Law Olmstead designed New York's Central Park to help refine and civilize the immigrant masses who had to be socialized to dominant WASP values. The first generation of European immigrants learned American culture in the special garden that was set aside for them. Their grandchildren do the same at the mall.

But at the same time that public parks were being built for these urban masses, new commercial space was also being devised for them, the department store. The shopping mall is an artful conflation of park and store. The shops and streets of the city enter the park, but the disorderly world of which they are a part does not. The self-control and temperance of the park are extended to the commercial aspects of the town, but this can only work if new kinds of rules are enforced that sanitize the street.

The relationship of the mall to the grandiose department stores of the late nineteenth and early twentieth centuries is obvious enough, but it is important to note a paradigm shift between those spaces and the contemporary mall. It is a shift from work and seriousness to fun and play. The semi-Gothic, cathedral-like John Wanamaker department store in downtown Philadelphia was built around a grand court, several stories high, at the center of which was a gigantic bronze statue of a resting eagle. Shoppers were invited to gather and rest around this figure. An equally monumental organ, complete with a wall of organ pipes, occupied one of the sides of the court on its upper floors and regularly filled the space with classical organ music. Shoppers were invited to listen. This is sacred space appropriated by the marketplace, the nineteenth-century model. The twentieth-century model is a mall like the one that stands on the site of the old Willow Grove Amusement Park in suburban Philadelphia. Some of its walls are covered with large photographs of the amusement park in its glory days, and reproductions of carousel horses and of other amusement park artifacts hang from the ceilings. Shoppers are invited to think about the previous history of the space, one form of amusement having been replaced by another. Where visitors once paid to shoot guns at plates, they now pay to buy plates; where they once drove kiddie cars and tried to keep them on the tracks, they now park grown-up cars; and where they once got lost in the fun house, they now get lost in Bloomingdale's. In the Gothic department store the shoppers were asked to see themselves in sacred, religious space. Shopping was worship. In the mall, shoppers are asked to see themselves in funland. Shopping is play. We are out of the church and into the garden. Play, of course, means many things. To Friedrich Schiller at the end of the eighteenth century play meant the ability to reconcile that which otherwise could not be reconciled, the real and the ideal, the finite and the infinite, the emotional and the rational. And this the mall certainly does. To the American anthropologist Clifford Geertz play—now called "deep play"—means the ways in which the members of a culture, in their leisure, learn the meanings of their culture. The mall fulfills this meaning of play, too.

And the garden did, too. William Kent, the foremost English landscape designer of the early eighteenth century, decorated the walls of one of his garden temples with scenes from Edmund Spenser's great epic poem *The Faerie Queene*. Visitors got to envision themselves as knights crossing allegorical fields of play. But there is at least one fundamental difference from Willow Grove worth noting here: the eighteenth-century citizen was reminded of his or her heroic past; the contemporary shopper is reminded of his or her past in funland. "To walk in a Renaissance garden is in fact to walk though the avenues of the Renaissance mind," Roy Strong writes in *The Renaissance Garden in England*. One might argue, similarly, that to walk in the shopping mall is to walk though the avenues of the twentieth-century mind. What we see are both the promises and the problems of commodified life. It is only a matter of learning how to read the meanings of the space.

CHAPTER 9

PLAYBOY and
THE BOOK OF THE COURTIER

lashboy occupies a unique position in the history of pornography in America: it is at once the most successful, the most respectable, and the most complex of girlie magazines, clean and dirty at the same time, radical and conservative, liberating and repressive, serious and profoundly ridiculous. By enveloping a striptease in an extraordinary glorification of consumer culture, then surrounding it with interviews, essays, and stories by and/or about contemporary figures and events, and finally dressing it up in a kind of ersatz wholesomeness, *Playboy* has created a peculiarly middle-class pornography. Hugh Hefner, to whom the credit for much of this incongruous mix of decency and indecency must go, is properly considered the Norman Rockwell of American pornographers. Or, to take a more jaundiced view, he is like the proprietor of the whorehouse in Nathanael West's darkly comic *A Cool Million*, who has decorated his rooms in a series of regional patriotic American motifs, the better to attract customers.

But this is to pass a value judgment on Hefner much too quickly and glibly, to speak of *Playboy* with disgust and ridicule before its meanings as a cultural text have been established. *Playboy* can just as easily be praised for its unique pornographic mix. In terms of Michel Foucault's critical history of sexuality, Hefner's magazine signifies a major shift in middle-class attitudes toward sexuality. "Decency and voluptuousness in its fullest acceptance cannot exist together, one would kill the other," the anonymous nineteenth-century author of *My Secret Life* argues (quoted in Charney, *Sexual Fiction*, 72). Hefner has neatly inverted this traditional attitude. And along with the inversion has come a new sexual image for the middle-class woman—in place of "the nervous woman, the frigid wife, [and] the indifferent mother," the types Foucault establishes in his archeology of nineteenth-century sexuality (*Introduction*, 110), we now have the happy, sexually "liberated" girl next door. This too is a cultural fabrication, of course, but as a fabrication of our own time and place it deserves careful examination.

Placed against other forms of discourse on the human body with which it has important parallels—the nude in the history of art, for example, as well as such inquiries into sexuality and manner as Herbert Marcuse's *Eros and Civilization* and Baldesar Castiglione's *Book of the Courtier*—Playboy can be seen as a much more complex and culturally significant text than it would appear when it is simply ridiculed as a preposterously unreal girlie magazine. In fact, *Playboy* is so much like *The Book of the Courtier*, which it repeats in intricate detail, that it deserves the same kind of close reading from literary and cultural critics.

Playboy is still a striptease. The naked and seminaked women posed in the magazine are shown almost exclusively as passive, childlike, and nondemanding, subject only to the sexual whims of the male reader. And although this is typical of pornography aimed at men, *Playboy* is striptease with a difference. In the classic striptease, a woman peels away layer after layer of exotic clothing, images that encourage the audience's sexual fantasies; in *Playboy*'s version it is the reader who must peel away page after page of exotic advertisement, undressing a fantasy image of a woman literally enveloped in images of other fantasy commodities, which themselves encourage the reader's sexual fantasies since they are complicated by their own erotic affect. These commodities now play a different role in the process: they are the goods in which the reader must dress himself in order to win over the woman. The elements of the classic striptease are all present; they have just been neatly, artfully rearranged in the interests of the American marketplace. This is a commodity fetishism of remarkable erotic power. Completely surrounded by consumer goods that create an erotic aura around him, the reader experiences the polymorphous perversity of the commodity fetish. The middle-class iconology is not trivial or accidental for Hefner, then, but a sign of the complex intertwinings of sexuality and economics, an indication that an entire economic system has learned how to turn a trick. *Playboy* is not pornography as we have known it before.

It is also something much more than pornography, a courtesy book or book of manners. The interviews, the advice columns, the short stories, and the essays, all of which come in addition to the erotic treatment of commodities, convert the striptease into a text that defines what it means to be a civilized man of a certain age and class in contemporary America. To be sure, these are the features that the horny adolescent reader may ignore in his rush to the pictures of semi-naked women, or see only peripherally, but the magazine has other readers who must stop and linger. "The text loads the image, burdening it with a culture, a moral, an imagination," Roland Barthes writes in "The Photographic Message" (26). By means of these overloaded images and their textual envelopes *Playboy* has differentiated itself from the competition, converting the girlie magazine into something more ambitious and powerful. The criticism of *Playboy* has concentrated on the ways in which the magazine manipulates images of women and their sexuality. Yet the magazine also manipulates images of men and their sexuality, perpetuating the consumer culture's domination of men, and, beyond that, it powerfully enunciates a code of manners for men and for women.

"I assume you drink Martell," an elegant woman says in an advertisement that appears in *Playboy*. She has turned and is facing the reader. There is, of course, only one answer that the male reader can offer—"Yes, of course I drink Martell. I've always drunk Martell." The ad makes obvious what is sometimes overlooked in the criticism of the magazine: women are not simply another *Playboy* accessory like the cars and the stereos. They are the rewards for the male who can learn the right behavior patterns and buy into the consumption ethic without hesitation. If you buy the goods, and along with it the pursuit of pleasure, and question nothing except what restricts your pleasure, you get the girl. It's a cross between *Let's Make a Deal* and *Faust*, with the always unreal fantasy woman as the bait and the male reader as the sucker who sells his soul, seduced by a sexual illusion. This male is a victim, someone who reads the magazine in a state of sexual semiarousal, anticipating the next fantasy image to appear and fantasizing about his contact with her, a condition that makes him

particularly vulnerable to the magazine's pornographic and extrapor-
nographic content.

The magazine shapes this content into something that approaches
a traditional narrative story. The *Playboy* formula, which varies little
from issue to issue, is like an illustrated coming-of-age novel with the
reader as hero, an ephebe who is apprenticed to a magnificent Don
Juan, Hefner himself. And it is as a contemporary repetition of Don
Juan that Hefner should be understood. The pornography provides
the major events of *Playboy*'s quasi-literary plot. The single most consistent feature of the magazine is a sequence of three sets of images of
nude women, the first of which is usually the most innocent and romantic, the last one of which is usually the most graphic and pornographic, and the one between them, the playmate of the month, the
one that is always the most complex, for it invariably combines innocence and nymphomania in an uneasy and powerful alliance. The
playmate feature is also the most detailed and intimate of the three
sets of images, with extensive photographs, a biographical data sheet,
and statements by the woman about her needs in a man. She is also
presented in the largest single nude image, the foldout. It is with this
woman that the reader achieves a certain kind of fantasy intimacy and
it is therefore both sexually and textually the climax of the story.

Following and elaborating on this pornographic sequence, the magazine produces a plot about sexual education, the ephebe's journey
from innocence to sophistication. The first part of the magazine, before the first nude feature, is devoted to building up the ephebe's confidence: the book, movie, and music reviews and the advice columns,
which give him knowledge, and the glossy advertisements for exaggeratedly male products, which give him models for ways of being in
the world—the tough outdoorsman, the sophisticated habitué of the
nightclub, the strong and virile athlete. Along with all this comes the
Playboy interview, the correlative to the playmate feature, which allows the ephebe a certain emotional intimacy with a real male role
model—a television star, a politician, a businessman, an athlete—who
has made it in the world. With his general confidence bolstered, the
ephebe is ready for his first meeting with a submissive and sexually
attractive woman, and the first pornographic feature quickly follows.
The magazine continues to build up the ephebe's knowledge of the
world after this first sexual experience with longer and more involved

essays about the perfect drink, the perfect football team, the perfect car, and the perfect gadget. And some of these pieces begin to elaborate on the problems of maintaining a *Playboy* lifestyle, marriage, divorce, aging.

And then the ephebe is upon the playmate of the month, the cute girl next door, an image from an Andy Hardy movie, except that she turns out to be driven by fantastic sexual passion, likes men who are almost exactly like the ephebe, and poses in provocative and remarkably explicit sexual positions for him. The adolescent male fantasy is confirmed. And although this fantasy could very well be intimidating to the still insecure ephebe—it is, after all, so perfect—the playmate herself is very reassuring. She is evidently as childlike and insecure as the ephebe himself. At the bottom of the data sheet are the pictures of the playmate as an ordinary kid, as if taken out of her family's photo album. The ephebe is being made welcome by the unseen family in this way, accepted as a suitor, and he is ready for the foldout, the playmate in all her sexual glory. Not every playmate is exactly the same, just almost the same. The power of the playmate feature—its combination of decency and indecency—is worth considering in detail. The sequence of these photographs of the playmate is often from very decent, to somewhat less decent, to somewhat pornographic, to very pornographic. The virgin becomes a whore before our eyes, but then the playmate data sheet serves to remind us that in some way she is still a virgin.

What follows the playmate feature is always a page of party jokes—after this fantasy coitus, some light entertainment. This is not the time to get serious or sad, for the reader cannot be allowed to grow too attached to this particular fantasy woman. He is now almost a man of the world, ready for his last trial, the visit to the whorehouse or its more contemporary variants, the wild sorority house or the Hollywood party. After several more essays there is the final section of nudity, often quite raw and graphic, sex without any pretense of intimacy, romance, or innocence—many women, sometimes masturbating themselves, always in compromising positions: page after page of sex stars of the year, of the year in sex, of the decade in sex, of the century in sex, of girls from assorted colleges and universities in standard whorehouse poses, of women naked together, of breasts and genitalia in close-up, of the life of a porn queen. The ephebe has become a man, his rite of passage is over. Today I am a Don Juan. And the magazine slowly winds down with continuations of stories, silly news items, but nothing substantial.

But the pornographic formula of the magazine itself is not silly. Defining the ars erotica of the non-Western tradition, Foucault explains that it depends on a special relationship between master and disciple, and what he says can be extended to the relationship between Hefner and the ephebe. "The relationship to the master who holds the secrets is of paramount importance; only he, working alone, can transmit this art in an esoteric manner and as the culmination of an initiation in which he guides the disciple's progress with unfailing skill and severity" (*Introduction*, 57). Hefner's version of this ars erotica is available in monthly installments at neighborhood magazine stands, but what is important is the extent to which it meets Foucault's definition of the non-Western way of handling sexuality, the way our society has rejected in favor of a scientific sexuality. Seen in this context, Hefner's pornography is not easy to dismiss or ridicule.

Playboy and the Sexual Tradition

Playboy can be placed in a number of traditions, but two appear to be the most important for an understanding of *Playboy*'s content. The first is the magazine's connection to the history of images of the nude in Western art, primarily in painting, the second to the history of philosophic speculation on love, sex, and manners. The context of art history returns us briefly to the meaning of the magazine's pornographic base. The standard study of the nude in Western art is Kenneth Clark's *The Nude: A Study in Ideal Form*, first delivered as a series of lectures in 1953, the same year that Hefner first published *Playboy*. Following Plato, Clark traces two different kinds of nudes in representational art from the Renaissance to the nineteenth century: sacred and profane, virgin and whore. These disappear for the most part in the twentieth century in Clark's history—but here *Playboy* provides a brilliant coda. In its three pornographic sequences, the magazine takes up Clark's clean and dirty nudes, presenting them singly and then in the playmate of the month, in brilliant combination. Clark's two great traditions do not disappear as he believes—they have simply moved from the walls of the museums of the world to the bedrooms of adolescent males. They are reproduced mechanically and have lost all of their original aura, but contain their original artistic elements.

Playboy's nudes, of course, appear to the magazine's critics as "artistic" in only the most shallow of ways—airbrushed, unreal, almost unnatural. This is not the way real women are, and therefore, we are told, the magazine is crass manipulation. And yet once the correspondence to the tradition of the nude in painting has been established, another perspective becomes possible. "We do not wish to imitate; we wish to perfect," Clark argues about nude representation. Photographs of the naked human body are not art, he explains. "We are immediately disturbed by wrinkles, pouches and other small imperfections which, in the classical scheme, are eliminated," and this, he suggests is because we have all "grown accustomed to the harmonious simplifications of antiquity" (*The Nude*, 4). Clark also insists that such perfected nudes are erotic. Here, it would seem, is where Hefner's nudes properly belong.

But it is the second tradition—that of the philosophic discourse on sex, love, and manners—that allows for the fullest understanding of *Playboy*'s power and importance. That tradition, which begins with Plato and extends to Foucault, presents a wide field of inquiry, and although *Playboy* can be read against any of this discourse, it is with Marcuse's *Eros and Civilization* and Castiglione's *Book of the Courtier* that *Playboy* can be most helpfully compared. *Eros and Civilization* originated in a series of lectures in 1950 and 1951, and was first published in 1955, again at approximately the time Hefner was creating *Playboy*. Both Marcuse and Hefner were reconsidering the relationship between eros and civilization, each advocating the pursuit of sexual pleasure outside of the bounds of monogamy and love, one as philosopher in an often theoretical text, one as pornographer in an often graphic text. And although they did not always agree, they should be seen as fellow travelers in the erotic revolution of the time. Neither was interested in the woman's perspective on all of this, but both admired what the woman meant as object of male desire. "The beauty of the woman, and the happiness she promises are fatal in the work-world of civilization," Marcuse wrote (*Eros*, 161), sounding like Hefner or at least one of his more thoughtful (and sexist) editors.

Marcuse wished to rescue sexuality from the repressions of civilization, and such a nonrepressive reality, he believed, was to be based on a kind of fantasy that he connected to Schiller's concept of play, with its ability to mediate between sensuousness and reason. "The play impulse is the vehicle of this liberation" (187). The parallels with Hefner and his magazine of play and fantasy are obvious. But Marcuse also warned that the forces of repression could take advantage of a new eroticism and turn it into a new kind of domination, that erotic play could be made into mindless leisure activities and "sexual liberty . . . harmonized with profitable conformity" (94). This could be a critique of *Playboy*, which happily embraced the relationship between civilization and eroticism, struggling only against the repression of pleasure. Marcuse and Hefner conceive of the same possibilities, but take different points of view about them and make different choices about what can or should be achieved. Hefner goes after sexual pleasure; Marcuse is not willing to abandon freedom. If we are to judge the texts by their impact on the culture at large, Hefner's alternative prevailed.

The Playboy and the Courtier

As a book of manners, *Playboy* is a contemporary variant on Castiglione's *Book of the Courtier*, the greatest of the courtesy books published during the Italian Renaissance. A long and carefully developed dialogue on the art of living as a courtier or as a court lady in an Italian city-state, *The Book of the Courtier* was written in 1514, published in 1528, and translated into English in 1561. Set at the court of the duke and duchess of Urbino, a city-state where Castiglione had once worked as a high-ranking member of the government, the book is an animated discussion by a number of articulate speakers and is loosely based on the model of a Platonic dialogue. Similarly, Hefner's *Playboy* is filled with stories, feature articles, advice columns, and interviews concerned with the art of living as a sexually active man. First published in 1953, it has always included sexually explicit photographs and glossy advertisements for expensive consumer products; *The Book of the Courtier*, published before the age of the cheap mechanical reproduction of images, contains no pornographic illustrations or advertisements for consumer products. This significant difference aside, *Playboy* is *The Book of the Courtier* adapted to the demands of American popular culture.

The Book of the Courtier has been judged a great work of literature and is taught regularly as one of the masterpieces of the Italian Renaissance. *Playboy* has been regularly denounced as pornography and as sexist propaganda. Illustrated with soft-core pornographic images of women, *Playboy* repeats most of the concerns of *The Book of the Courtier*. It is unlikely that the editors of *Playboy* have done this deliberately—the literature of the high Renaissance is hardly their forte—rather, in responding to the needs of their audience they have produced a slick magazine that is in most essential respects identical to the detailed and thoughtful discourse Castiglione created in the early sixteenth century in response to the needs of his audience. The needs of these two audiences appear to be extremely similar.

The Book of the Courtier is a discourse between a series of male and female speakers, Castiglione's friends in the city of Urbino, who participate in a Neoplatonic dialogue on the nature of the perfect courtier and his companion, the perfect court lady. Although these speakers bear the names of real historical figures with whom Castiglione was acquainted in Urbino, in his dialogue they are idealized, made over into art. Their conversations are presented as an entertainment, a game played with wit and cleverness on four consecutive evenings at court. And although the men have the predominant voice in this dialogue, the presence of the women is always a factor—the duchess of Urbino has arranged it and intervenes at key moments. The speakers argue with each other, sometimes gently, sometimes with considerable vehemence. The discourse itself, divided into four books, builds from relatively simple subjects to far more complex topics, beginning with points about the courtier's ability to bear arms, ride a horse, excel at sports such as tennis, and play musical instruments, continuing with his air of personal confidence, his grace, his ability to manage impressions, and his responsibilities to his prince, and concluding with his relationships with women and their various meanings for him, from sensual pleasure to pure truth. It is here that the dialogue gets most heated: some of Castiglione's male speakers fear women and their passion while others are willing to grant women nearly equal status with men. From arguments about sex and sex roles, the speakers turn to defining the perfect court lady and her characteristics. The dialogue also includes a lengthy section on laughter and humor, numerous stories about the constancy or inconstancy of women, and culminates in a long Neoplatonic oration on the philosophic meaning of woman's beauty and the importance of renouncing mere sexual desire for a higher rational contact with ideal truth and ideal beauty. That contact, Castiglione's most sophisticated speaker, Pietro Bembo, insists, is entirely visual—the man looking at but not actually touching the woman. "Beauty can in no way be enjoyed, nor can the desire it excites in our minds be satisfied through the sense of touch," he argues, "but only by way of that sense whereof this beauty is the true object, namely, the faculty of sight" (*Book of the Courtier*, 347). If the courtier is content to look at the beautiful woman and not touch her, "he will feed his soul on the sweetest food . . . without passing to any unchaste appetite through desire for the body" (347).

The parallels with *Playboy* are significant. Like *The Book of the Courtier*, the magazine is also a dialogue between speakers, most of them male, who gather in this monthly format around the editor and founder, Hugh Hefner. His world of mansions, where his friends, we are asked to believe, sometimes do gather, is as unreal as Castiglione's Urbino. And his writers, like Castligione's speakers, are again at pains to define the perfect playboy and his companion, the playmate. Again the men have the predominant voice, although the presence of women is also a factor—not an idealized duchess but an idealized playmate, whom they also wish to please. Like the duchess, she is given some limited voice in the discourse. And again there is a play frame over the entire discourse. There would appear to be much less argument between the speakers than in *The Courtier*, although in fact there is a surprising amount of disagreement, enough to constitute a true debate on fundamental issues. And like *The Courtier*, the discourse itself builds from the obvious to the more subtle and complex, from the reviews and advice columns to the interviews, the longer essays and stories, and the nudes. There are jokes, cartoons, and more stories about the constancy or inconstancy of women. The contact between reader and playmate is entirely visual, of course, the man looking at but not actually touching the woman. Castiglione's Bembo would be discouraged but not appalled by this pornographic variation on Platonism. Voyeurism wasn't what he had in mind—and yet there is an intriguing possibility that *Playboy* is at the very first stage of a Neoplatonic ascent to the ideal of truth and beauty, something that becomes clear when Bembo's speech can be examined in detail. There is even a corresponding speech about sight in *Playboy*. "We men are visual down to our genetic code," Asa Berger writes in his "Men" column. "Telling us not to look at something is like telling us not to breathe. For the healthy male, looking is living" ("Men," December 1985, 47).

Some of the correspondences between the two texts do reveal significant difference: the courtier is advised to master arms, excel at horsemanship, participate in sports, and play musical instruments. The playboy is advised to know about cars, to identify the best football players, to be familiar with the best films and musical albums. The difference is between doing and knowing. The courtier participates. The playboy is a voyeur, a spectator. But most of the correspondences reveal similarity. The courtier is advised "to practice in all things a certain *sprezzatura*," defined as faked nonchalance, "so as to conceal all art and make whatever is done or said appear to be without effort and almost without any thought about it" (*Courtier*, 43). The playboy, a master of "cool" and "unruffled" detachment (Cox, "Sex and Secularization," 174), is praised for absolute confidence in the face of whatever comes his way, called in one essay "The Fine Art of Cocksurety" (February 1985, 85). The courtier is advised to dress according to the custom of the majority, but in general to wear dark and generally conservative clothing (*Courtier*, 120–22). So is the playboy, to whom the magazine offers a consistent selection of similar fashion. The courtier has a delicate relationship to maintain with his prince, who may sometimes ask him to perform improper acts—"In dishonorable things we are not bound to obey anyone" (117). The playboy has an equally delicate relationship with certain laws of the culture that restrict his pleasures, and those he neither respects nor obeys. In this way the playboy and the courtier are opposites.

The speakers in *The Book of the Courtier* argue with each other much of the time, and sometimes there is no consensus, requiring readers to choose for themselves. The speakers in *Playboy* do the same. The magazine is a mix of contradictory voices and contradictory advice, through which the reader must make his own way. The September 1994 issue is typical. One writer bashes homosexuality in a letter to the *Playboy* advisor while David Geffen, the subject of the *Playboy* interview, speaks with pride about his own homosexuality, and another feature praises bisexual women as the true leaders of the sexual revolution. Geffen disparages materialism while the rest of the magazine celebrates the joys of materialism with articles on expensive clothes and video equipment. The magazine takes a generally liberal line on social problems, but an essay praising graphic sex and violence in the media is almost immediately followed by another advocating greater use of the death penalty. The various voices in the magazine undercut each other, as do the voices in *The Book of the Courtier*.

Both the courtier and the playboy are more interested in women than any other single topic. In Castiglione the speakers debate whether women are superior or inferior to men, or simply different; whether they are driven by strong sexual passions; whether they should be respected, seduced, or both; whether it is better to possess a woman's body, her mind, or both, and in what order. When these men consider the ideal court lady, they advise her not to allow herself to be seduced, but at such an idea they laugh most heartily and have to remind themselves that they are not discussing reality, only defining an ideal (264). And they have very practical advice for would-be courtiers, of the sort that belongs in the *Playboy* advisor. "Since men dry out more than women in the act of procreation, it frequently happens that they do not keep their vitality as long as women," one explains (219). In a comparable passage from *Playboy* the editor explains to a woman how she might get her husband interested in foreplay. "Women who are begged refuse to yield to the one who begs them," another of Castiglione's speakers explains, "and those who are not begged do the begging themselves" (244). The *Playboy* advisor tells a man to stop being a perfect gentleman with women, to become forceful and assertive.

The longest speech on women in Castiglione, delivered by Bembo near the end of the discourse, calls into question everything previously spoken on the subject. Praising the joys of platonic love, he warns "whoever thinks to enjoy that beauty by possessing the body deceives himself, and is moved not by a true knowledge through rational choice, but by false opinion through sensual appetite: wherefore the pleasure that is consequent upon this is necessarily false and mistaken" (337). Men who "satisfy their unchaste desires with the woman they love" either suffer from boredom or come to despise the woman they have seduced. From both, Bembo argues, they are driven to seek to repeat the experience with other women, but after their momentary passions "they never feel anything save anguish, torments, sorrows, sufferings, toils" (338). He forgives this kind of behavior in young men, driven by their "vigor of flesh and blood" (339), because "although sensual love is bad at every age, yet in the young it deserves to be excused, and in some sense is perhaps permitted" (340). It may incite them to "do worthy acts." But he condemns such behavior in men old enough to know better. "But if, even when they are old, they keep the fire of the appetites in their cold hearts . . . like senseless fools they deserve with perpetual infamy to be numbered among the unreasoning animals" (340). Hefner, now aging fast, sometimes pictured in his pajamas in the magazine, other times surrounded by fields of naked young women, stands in sharp contrast with Bembo's ideal. "The continual contemplation of beauty in the body often perverts sound judgment," Bembo warns (350). Here it would seem is a crucial difference between the two texts. *The Book of the Courtier* elevates the discourse at the end and preaches against the hot-blooded sexual passion that has characterized many of the earlier speakers. It is something to outgrow.

Playboy has this same philosophical coda even if it is not obvious to many of its readers. The great majority of the short fiction in *Playboy* functions in a way that is very similar to Bembo's dialogue in *The Courtier*, undercutting, calling into question, and otherwise negating the adolescent sexuality that the magazine seems so obviously to be promoting. These stories regularly attack *Playboy*'s treatment of women, its famous imagery of the perfect female body, its preoccupation with sex, its concept of nudity, and its notion of male domination of women. Consider these two examples, which represent a much larger sample. A wealthy and powerful older man finds himself at a nightclub with two sexy and much younger women. Recently divorced and only dimly troubled by the fact that these women are young enough to be his daughters, he can't believe his good luck. We are in his mind as he gets progressively drunker and more sexually aroused by them, as "his hard-on the size of a bowling pin" drains "all the blood from his faltering brain." The portrait is far from complimentary. He has all the usual *Playboy* fantasies, which are elaborated in great pornographic detail, but these no longer seem particularly attractive or appropriate here. The old man only becomes increasingly repulsive and pathetic, worried that he will wet his pants, and when he gets one of the women's earrings painfully attached to his ear, he rushes off to a hospital emergency room concerned only that someone will recognize him (Joyce Carol Oates, "What I Lived For," September 1994, 154). The story could have been written by Bembo.

He could have written this one as well: at a time when aliens from other worlds have begun visiting the earth as tourists, a shady Swiss art dealer is making big profits by illegally selling them the earth's great artistic treasures. But then one night at a bar that caters to these tourists in Morocco, he becomes fascinated by an alien who has dressed for its visit to earth in a manufactured earth-woman body. This is the *Playboy* magazine ideal of woman. "She looked like . . . something that belonged to a 3-D billboard, one of those unreal, idealized women who turn up in ads for cognac or skiing holidays." He desires the woman even after he understands it is mechanical, that inside is something like a long green lizard, even after he understands that this desire will compromise his business ventures. He offers the alien a million dollars for its sexual favors, and is accepted. His performance as a lover "might well have been the finest of his life" but it responds like the inflatable woman balloon it is, and "lay there like a wax doll." Worse yet, he begins to understand that the alien is watching, studying him—he is the sex object, not it. Then, as his frustration is about to give way to despair, the alien gives him a taste of its planet's brand of sexuality, and a powerful mental image of the beauty of its planet's landscape overcomes all his senses. He is overwhelmed. So compelling is this alien sex that he doesn't even care that he has lost money in the process and along with it his business partner, who doesn't care to mix business and pleasure. When the story ends he has decided to hang out at bars that cater to aliens and seek out other kinds of alien sex. Each tourist might offer something even more extraordinary (Robert Silverberg, "Tourist Trade," December 1984). The two great values of the magazine—having a lot of money and having sex with a lot of women—are here shown to be incompatible. There is, further, the warning that once you get truly hooked on sex, you are destined to spend the rest of your life looking for pickups at bars at the end of the universe. Finally, and most subversive of the *Playboy* philosophy, we are shown that sex with a fantasy image is sex with an inflatable dummy, but sex with a very ugly and repulsive creature can be fantastic. It's a brilliant and creative response to the basic tenets of the magazine. There are many other examples, but these two will serve. "Discourse transmits and produces power," Foucault writes, "it reinforces it, but also undermines and exposes it, renders it fragile and makes it possible to thwart it" (*Introduction*, 101).

Nudes

There is one extremely obvious difference between the two texts—the absence of images of nude women in *The Book of the Courtier*. Writing before the age of the mechanical reproduction of images, Castiglione had no opportunity to include them. But were we to turn to the nudes painted in the Renaissance, including those by Castiglione's friend Raphael, we would get an idea of the corresponding Renaissance images of women, and these turn out to be reasonably close to *Playboy*'s. The magazine's impossibly idealized and airbrushed nudes are regularly criticized for their lack of reality, but they are not reality, of course. And in the long history of the nude, they are closest to the nudes of the Renaissance. There are many Renaissance nudes to consider, the *Portrait of the Fornarina*, for example, until fairly recently attributed to Raphael, which is a painting of a nude girl, seated, who is clutching a see-through cloth to her upper body, hiding little, or Raphael's version of *The Three Graces*, after a standard medieval subject, which shows three views of the nude female body. Kenneth Clark writes of this picture: "These sweet, round bodies are as sensuous as strawberries, and although their attitude must be derived from art, their power to please us is owing to a grasp of nature" (103). Sometimes the correspondences between Renaissance and modern are quite precise: Botticelli's famous nude, the *Birth of Venus*, serves as the model for the cover of the March 1984 issue of *Playboy*, which shows a sexy young woman with long hair flowing over her body, her hands covering her genitalia.

Following Erwin Panofsky's analysis of the aesthetic theory of the Renaissance as both faithfulness to the real appearance of things and, at the same time, an idealization of these appearances, Wayne Rebhorn has shown the elimination of "particularizing details" in *The Courtier* (*Courtly Performance*, 83). Renaissance paintings and Castiglione's characterizations are idealizations of real people, he argues, which make sure that "ideal figures possess the illusory appearance of life" (84). "Idealization also meant to some degree the identification of the particular individual as a type. This identification was maintained even in portraiture" (74). This would seem to describe Hefner's nudes fairly closely. "To create works both real and ideal which expressed generalized, universal, spiritual states while possessing rational order—this was the problem that confronted artists at the end of the fifteenth century" (65). Hefner's nudes meet all of these criteria save one—they have little to do with spiritual states, unless we are willing to grant, with Foucault, that sex has become our religion. In a letter to Castiglione, whose portrait he had painted, Raphael wrote:

"to paint a beauty, I would have to see many beautiful women, with the added condition, that your excellency would be with me to choose the best. But since there is a lack both of good judges and of beautiful women here, I make use of a certain Idea which comes into my mind" (quoted in Rebhorn, 62). Again, the description fits Hefner's universalized female figure. These descriptions of the art of Castiglione's own time allow Hefner's nudes to be seen in an entirely different way. They are a peculiar anachronism, a return to the aesthetic ideals of the Renaissance at a time when nudes are no longer being painted in what one could call conventional realism. They are thus the same kind of repetition of Raphael or Titian as the text itself is of Castiglione. In *Ways of Seeing* John Berger compares various nudes painted by Rubens and Bronzino, among others, with the photographs of nudes in modern girlie magazines and concludes that "the essential way of seeing women, the essential use to which their images are put, has not changed" (64).

Both *The Book of the Courtier* and *Playboy* are texts that meet Foucault's requirement for inclusion in the history of sexual discourse. Both are explicitly about sex and power, one somewhat more graphically than the other. Both are about "those intentional and voluntary actions by which men not only set themselves rules of conduct, but also seek to transform themselves, to change themselves into their singular being, and to make their life into an oeuvre that carries certain aesthetic values and meets certain stylistic criteria" (Foucault, *Uses of Pleasure*, 10–11). The two texts are not the same, of course. The playboy has no prince to advise, is not in training for important government service, does not matter in the same terms in which the courtier matters. But their similarities are more significant. "The history of sexuality supposes two ruptures," Foucault writes, the first in the seventeenth century with the "advent of the great prohibitions" and the second in the twentieth century, "the moment when the mechanisms of repression were seen as beginning to loosen their grip" (*Introduction*, 115). These texts fit into this history very well, the first coming before the prohibitions, the second after their lifting. The two texts are thus the same for good reason: the history of sexuality has come full circle.

CHAPTER 10

COSMOPOLITAN and the Woman's Coming-of-Age Novel

Cosmopolitan is a contemporary female bildungsroman, an illustrated, commercialized, and fragmented woman's coming-of-age novel in which the reader herself functions as heroine, making her way selectively through the typical crises of late adolescence and early adulthood that the text presents to her. It is also a romance, a love story melodramatically simplified and erotically idealized, marked by a descent into a dream world. And it is a novel of manners, devoted to the translation of social gesture, dress, look, and public behavior into explicit meaning and concerned with the individual's relationship to social convention. What may appear to be a superficial conduct book for young women presented within a massive envelope of advertising is the adaptation of established literary forms to the demands of altered economic, social, and aesthetic realities. Cosmopolitan is a significant modification of the literary traditions to which it belongs, since it is now about a woman's experience within a consumer-oriented mass society. Thus this new mix of genres is appropriately commercialized, fragmented, repetitious, inconsistent, and vividly illustrated—Goethe as revised by Jane Austen, transformed by the commodity market, and then restructured by the Dadaists—but it retains the essential elements of the older literary forms: the concern with psychological growth and development over time, the interest in courtship and sexual behavior, the sense of an emerging coherent self, the problems of mastering social convention.

The result is something akin to Jane Austen's *Sense and Sensibility* in the age of mechanical reproduction, a text now without any literary aura, repeated every month with minor variations, that takes the characters, issues, and plot of the Austen novel and of related stories in the genres—Edith Wharton's *House of Mirth* and Gustave Flaubert's *Madame Bovary* are important precursor texts as well—and transforms them into Dadaist collage. It is, then, a brilliant modernist text, what would have resulted if Marcel Duchamp had thrown a hand grenade into the great courtship novels of the nineteenth and early twentieth centuries, then pasted the fragments together. It is at the same time the most familiar and ordinary of mass cultural texts, beneath the contempt, let alone the attention, of literary critics. Appropriately, the traditional author has disappeared in this modernist mass-cultural collage, and in her place is the commercial marketplace, all the advertisers, editors, writers, and readers that make up a collectivist enterprise of completely inartistic intention, which has, for reasons that are clearly extremely important, nevertheless produced a text that repeats the essential elements of traditional literary forms.

Of all the women's magazines on the market, *Cosmopolitan* is the magazine that most closely approximates the content of the great courtship novels of the modern period, and on those grounds alone the comparison makes sense—although *Glamour* is somewhat similar. Examined superficially, the way we would never allow students to read a work of literature, *Cosmopolitan* does seem embarrassingly superficial. The articles listed on the cover, such as "Married to One Man, Having Sex with Another" (May 1994) or "One Girl's Plan to Meet and Marry a Millionaire (Who Isn't a Creep)" (March 1994), do not promise the depth we associate with a great novel. But this is only to read the teasing words on the cover, not the text itself, and although any individual essay in the magazine may present a very limited perspective on human life, the magazine itself is a collection of many different kinds of one-dimensional pieces, in which each writer's voice is only part of the heteroglossia of the text, a limited voice, that of a single character in a novel. If we do not fault *Madame Bovary* because the sexist and simplistic Rudolphe is the reigning authority on female eroticism within the text, neither should we fault *Cosmopolitan* for the limitations of any of its individual speakers. It is greater than the sum of its parts.

Not all of the traditional elements of the bildungsroman, romance, and novel of manners forms are present in any single issue of *Cosmopolitan*, nor are they necessarily arranged in chronological order, but the cumulative effect of many issues is to make the genres clear. Everything is finally present except for the chronological structure. Advertisements about seductions made possible by consumer products, essays about depression, divorce, and financial management, advice columns about making friends, stories about managing career and family, interviews with film stars, all of these present the reader with the elements from which a number of stories can be constructed. One makes sense of these fragments by seeing them as sequences in a life history. Their arbitrary presentation, the lack of coherent chronological sequence, seems puzzling until one considers another characteristic of these fragments—their lack of internal consistency. Alternately fantastic and realistic, naive and sophisticated, vivid and banal, patriarchal and feminist, the fragments can be arranged to produce individual stories of different meanings, one about a plain woman who embraces traditional values, another about a sexy, strong woman who delights in manipulating men on their own terms, and others about women who mix elements of both these extremes. Both characteristics of these fragments—their lack of sensible order and their lack of internal consistency—encourage the reader, indeed require her, to read and retain selectively in order to make sense of the text. In adapting the older genres to its own times, *Cosmopolitan* has created a participatory literary form, which the reader must recover, understand, and assemble according to her own individual needs. It becomes her story. Thus the contemporary text is not so much a degenerate version of the older models, but the creation of a much more involving emotional form in which the reader becomes the author of the text. In this respect *Cosmopolitan* resembles the avant-garde art of the mid twentieth century, which, according to Umberto Eco, is characterized by a radical openness and is made up of small units that must be arranged by each different performer, reader, viewer, or auditor. Eco praises this art form because it does not mask the fragmentary state of our lives with an outdated narrative convention but "reproduces the very ambiguity of our being-in-the-world" (*Open Work*, 153). So does *Cosmo*.

The magazine does not appear to be ambiguous at all. Nothing, for example, could be more obvious or one-dimensional than the woman on the cover. Aged between sixteen and twenty-five and posed in flashy clothing, she changes little from month to month, sometimes

revealing breast or thigh, always looking out with eyes that communicate her own knowledge of her sexual power: "I may appear to be
a sex object for men," she says in this way, "but I know what I am
doing. I have learned that sexuality is power." She is a student, one
might say, of Nietzsche and Foucault. One remarkable cover (October
1984) shows the woman wearing unusual earrings in the shape of a
man dangling upside down and hanging by his testicles. She may show
such Nietzschean ressentiment from time to time, the ressentiment of
the weak, since she accepts male domination (grudgingly) and is after
only the kind of limited power it offers her. Thus she is almost exactly
like Flaubert's Emma Bovary, Wharton's Lily Bart, and Austen's various heroines, who are all forced to make surface accommodations to
a society commanded by men. More successful than these earlier heroines in many respects—in her demands for sexual pleasure, in her
negotiations during courtship, and above all in her understanding of
how to manipulate what she is unwilling or unable to change—she
nevertheless pays her own price for all this. She grows as a person in
limited ways, and pleasing, tricking, or manipulating a man must always be on her mind. This may not be surprising, but what is surprising is that these and other weaknesses are often pointed out within
the magazine itself. The cover girl who seems so self-assured in her
display of sexual power is often shown within the magazine to be
precisely the wrong kind of woman, doomed to unhappiness or even
fatality, like Emma Bovary. "Is That All There Is? A Model's Glam-
orous Life and Tragic Death" (November 1989, 260), for example,
concerns such a woman who had been the model on the cover of an
earlier issue. What begins with a visual image of a woman that combines Foucault and Nietzsche develops into a full-blown investigation
of the meanings of the image for women.

Almost every position the magazine takes in its essays, stories, and
even in its advertising images is effectively countered by other sets of
essays, stories, and images. Image is undercut, negated by counter-
image, with the result that contrasting sets of messages about sex and
love, family and career are presented to the reader, which she must
either choose from or experience as absolute contradictions. Essays
that endorse women who lead sexually promiscuous lives alternate
with articles that endorse monogamous marriage and traditional family life. Stories that describe the ways in which women use sexuality
to gain fame, fortune, or power are followed by stories that stress the

importance for women of accepting greatly diminished expectations, both sexually and psychologically. And statements by the leaders of contemporary feminism are undercut by essays and stories that attack the basic values of feminism, and vice versa. The magazine offers its readers distinct choices between differing models of behavior and, within those models, between certain sexual, personal, and psychological values. Individuals can find very different sets of messages within the magazine by reading selectively or they can assess the relative merits of these different values by reading more inclusively.

Reading *Cosmopolitan*

The primary subject of the magazine is the psychosexual development of women between the ages of eighteen and twenty-five, and although the content comes in random order, it is easy enough to recover the sequence: We move from "The Fun of Flirting" (March 1992, 78) to "How to Handle a Brand-New Man" (October 1994, 82) and "How to Close the Deal (Get Married)" (February 1989, 170). From "Lovemaking: The First Time" (January 1985, 72) and "The Newlywed's Guide to Love on the First Night" (October 1985, 146) we progress to "Settling In: When the Newness Wears Off" (September 1983, 102), "I'm Pregnant: Do I Look Excited?" (November 1989, 198), and "When Heartbreak Hits" (May 1992, 104). What follows is "Crazy Time: The Aftermath of Divorce" (January 1983, 177) and "I Don't Want Him, You Can't Have Him—When Your Ex Remarries" (October 1994, 230). A new cycle begins again with "You Can Be Single and Live a Rich, Full Life" (September 1994, 186). This is the basic structure of the text, which the magazine elaborates with other materials—the interviews with celebrities, the short surveys, the pseudoquizzes, and the fashion and cooking features—all of which are concerned with moving the woman forward along this sequence. Essays about "What Is This Thing Called a Nervous Breakdown?" (May 1994, 164) and "Stalking: The Nightmare That Never Ends" (April 1994, 198) indicate that forward movement along the sequence is not without its serious difficulties. We are involved in the core issues that a woman faces as a woman in contemporary society, all of which revolve around intimacy.

If the traditional subject of the bildungsroman is the psychological growth and development of a culturally representative young man

from childhood to adulthood, *Cosmopolitan* presents a greatly trun-
cated version of this story in the growth and development of a generalized young woman, yet what remains has obvious connections to
the original form. The typical plot of the bildungsroman concerns the
life of a young man as he moves from country to city, with a focus on
his career, his love affairs, and his general experience of urban life.
Cosmopolitan animates its developmental sequence with essays and
stories about young women who move from small town to big city,
prepare for their careers, and experience romance.

Upon this bildungsroman structure the magazine layers its other
two genres, romance and the novel of manners—versions of fantasy
and realism, the pleasure principle and the reality principle, respectively—which coexist in uneasy alliance within the magazine. The romance is the most obvious because it is the fundamental component
of most of the advertising, the content that accounts for two-thirds of
the magazine's pages and nearly all of its most striking visual imagery—indeed, a case can be made that this is the magazine's most
important content—and it is further supported by some of the magazine's regular features, particularly the fashion and clothing pieces,
the physical makeover stories, and the cover. The novel of manners—
the other story, which often works against the romance—exists much
more quietly in advice columns, interviews, and features, and although
it is also present in some of the advertising, it is much less glitzy and
therefore considerably harder to see, especially against the glamour
and sexual elaborations of the romance. This romance, in full-page,
full-color representations carefully crafted to play upon the reader's
own fantasies of perfect beauty and perfect sex, and concentrated in
the early parts of the magazine, begins with images of clean, healthy,
and innocent faces, with images of women touching soaps and mois-
turizers, all of which offer the reader a clean, fresh start. These soon
give way to images of women involved in all the various stages of
sexual anticipation, preparation, and intimacy. Innocence soon gives
way to experience. Impossibly beautiful and lithe young women pose
in elegant evening clothes, in underwear, in jeans, or naked, walking
on impossibly perfect white sandy beaches, waiting pensively in impossibly beautiful gardens, embracing impossibly handsome and lithe
young men. The liquor they pour into elegant crystal glasses flows in
the shape of flowers; the cigarettes they hold in their hands are smoke-

free; the Skin Perfecting Creme, Renewal Night Treatment, Active Daily Moisturizer, and Wrinkle Defense Cream that they massage on their faces work so perfectly that their complexions are flawless. Frozen in postures of erotic glory, like the images on Keats's well-wrought urn, these women will be forever fresh, clean, at the very peak of their sexual lives, clutching their MasterCards, fondling their jewelry and an assortment of men. Along with these images come words—*opium* (a fragrance), *passion* (a perfume), *obsession* (a perfume), *secret* (a deodorant), *carefree* (a panty shield), and above all *romance*: "Romance. It's dangerous, all-consuming. When it's in my life, it is my life. Le Jardin de Max Factor is the fragrance that captures the essence of romance and leaves me vulnerable," Jane Seymour tells us (November 1989). This is a reasonable summary of the *Cosmopolitan* romance: illogical, dreamlike, captivating. They want for nothing, these women, since all they desire is ageless physical beauty and endless sexual liaisons with similar kinds of men, and these turn out to be easily achievable through small but endless consumer purchases. As manipulation, this is an overwhelmingly powerful way to sell certain consumer products of dubious value, for by encouraging and directing the reader's fantasy life, which cannot ever be satisfied, a limitless demand is created. As story, this imagery reproduces the basic structure of literary romance.

Just as literary romance typically shows courtship through scenes of love at first sight and sexual ecstasy, the *Cosmopolitan* romance is filled with advertisements that center upon such moments of timeless emotional and sexual transport as provided by consumer products— the romance of capitalism could hardly be any different. But although love is the most important element of this romance form, confusion or loss of identity is at its core, and this appears in the *Cosmopolitan* romance as well, since the fragments of the story come in random order and in each the woman changes, is someone else. In literary romance, this loss of identity has been compared to entering an erotic dream state, and in the *Cosmopolitan* romance everything is intensely erotic and dreamlike. Images of reflecting pools, mirrors, pictures, tapestries, and statues appear in literary romance, where they are signs of the heroine's descent into dream experience. The heroine exchanges her identity for that of her shadow or reflection. The *Cosmopolitan* romance is similarly filled with images of women looking into mirrors, posed in front of tapestries and paintings, or even made over into lush and ornate paintings and sculptures themselves. Certainly the experience of reading *Cosmopolitan*—the reader now as heroine—is such a descent into a controlled erotic fantasy, for as she opens the pages of the magazine she is invited to exchange her identity for another, the reflection of the sexier and dreamlike woman whom the magazine holds up to her gaze. These are not only the ambiguities or contradictions of great art, but the nuances of *Cosmopolitan* as well. A woman in a L'Oréal advertisement peers ambiguously into a mirror. She is in profile and in complete darkness, except for the light reflected by the mirror that plays upon her eyes, creating an eerie mask of light. But her hand, holding the mirror, is pitch dark, and therefore the light source comes mysteriously from the mirror; mirror and lamp are the same. She notices something unusual—"Suddenly my lashes were a mile long," she tells us (February 1989, 26–27), but what the reader of the magazine must see is both the eyes in the intense light and the face in the intense dark, essential and endangered versions of the self, and the magic mirror that makes the vision possible. The consumer product the model grasps is a very trivial part of the drama before us.

Against this romance, the fantasy driven by pleasure, is the much more reality-driven novel of manners, the story of the young woman awkwardly mastering the various rules of modern urban life. She has very practical problems. She must learn about the nature of the workplace and how to survive it; how to understand her boss ("Boss Talk: What Your Boss Is Trying to Tell You," November 1989, 146); how to appear to be a good worker ("How to Look Busy Even When Doing Your Nails," March 1988, 234); how to deal with her coworkers ("Swimming with Sharks: When Your Colleagues Are Out for Blood," March 1994, 74); and finally, how to master the real skills that will one day make it possible for her to become the boss ("Top Women Executives Reveal Their Secrets for Success," June 1989, 224). In case she fails, she must learn how to start all over again ("You're Fired! What You Need Now Is a Survival Guide," April 1994, 210). She must also learn how to present herself in public, faking it when necessary ("Pass Yourself Off as a Woman of Wealth," October 1984, 178), and how to appear reasonably well educated ("How to Visit a Museum," October 1985, 194, and "Going for Baroque: A Guide to Classical Music," October 1984, 148). But what she must really learn, given the sexist nature of the text, is how to find a man, and here the story becomes one of real struggle, the first jolt of which comes immediately after the glorious opening sections of the advertisement romance, in what the magazine calls "Irma Kurtz's Agony Column." Kurtz, who looks like someone's loving mother and nothing at all like the women in the advertising romance, gets to answer the semi-articulate cries presumably written by the magazine's readers. "I'm a sophomore in college and get easily run-down and depressed. I have little confidence in myself" (March 1988, 76). "I caught my husband masturbating last week, and it upset me so much I've been unable to make love to him ever since" (November 1991, 42). "My best friend has suddenly turned gay! . . . Devastated, I cried for days. What am I to do?" (May 1994, 50). The advice the magazine offers is often sensible and calming: Look at your life more carefully, see a therapist, go slowly, don't be so hard on yourself. Although specific answers are often presented (accept yourself for who you are, don't put up with abuse from men, and never do anything just to get or keep a man), the general line is "Nothing in this life is easy" (December 1988, 76). But, of course, it *is* easy in the advertising romance.

And other features of the magazine as romance have told the reader just as insistently not to be herself. "The important point is that we not confuse fantasy with fact," another *Cosmopolitan* piece explains, although other parts of the magazine encourage this confusion ("What Fantasies Can Do for You," December 1988, 102). Pieces scattered throughout the magazine ask the reader to face reality and learn the ways of the world. "How to Stop Looking for Someone Perfect and Find Someone to Love" (January 1985), for example, tells the young woman to discard the magazine's romance fantasy altogether and accept her ordinary life and the ordinary men she already knows. One of them will do fine. Still, the romance has something to teach her, since she can put into play at least part of the sexual ethic it advocates. The advice in "How to Make an Impact on a Man" (February 1989, 174) is quite blunt: "Catch a man's eye and then very deliberately look down at his crotch. This should be done with a playful look or smile, not as though you're about to put him through a meat grinder. He should feel deliciously flattered, not attacked" (177). The heroine of the novel of manners who begins as a confused neophyte learns rather quickly the ways of the world. But things can get much grimmer, and at the very end of the magazine another series of advertisements appears, now small, gritty, and altogether different from those of the romance, for bust developers, mail-order secretarial schools, and pep and energy pills, tools for those who have not yet found anything else to be effective. This is the advertising version of the agony column, the other low point of the magazine, and it is here, on this note, that the text ends. What starts out like *Vogue* ends like *The National Enquirer* as the consumerist message reveals itself as an empty promise, and idealized images first of innocence and then of experience give way finally to images of despair, degenerating in front of us in a progression that perfectly repeats the final plot developments of *Madame Bovary* and *The House of Mirth*.

There are lessons in manners on almost every page of *Cosmopolitan*, representations of gesture, speech, decoration, and dress. The standard concerns of the novel of manners—courtship and marriage, exclusion and acceptance into social groups, class conflict and economic status—are the standard concerns of *Cosmopolitan*. "The Perils of Loving a Poor Man" (November 1985, 306) cautions against such a foolhardy idea as crossing class lines, but "Marrying Down: Would You Be Up to It?" (December 1988, 212) suggests that certain kinds of women (those who enjoy sex, those able to ignore social pressure) actually can do better by marrying down because working-class men have fewer sexual hang-ups and their bodies are in much better working condition. "Marrying Up: An American Dream—and Reality" (January 1984, 164) wholeheartedly endorses the idea and offers practical advice about how to achieve it, but "The Search: One Cosmo Girl's Plan to Meet (and Maybe Marry!) a Millionaire" (March 1994) warns that rich men are impossible. Novels of manners "show the relation between the individual and social convention to be more serious, more difficult, more dense and demanding than the central characters had expected" (Lindberg, *Edith Wharton*, 4). So, too, does *Cosmopolitan*. On the one hand there are the pieces that invite the reader to flout convention: A woman boasts about "My Affair with My Best Friend's Son" (January 1984, 88); another that "I Married My Live-In Baby-Sitter" (September 1983, 180); another, a divorced mother of two, gains a little extra income and a great deal of pleasure from seducing twenty-year-old men. "I'm not a prostitute," she tells us: "I prefer to think I'm helping people" ("What I Taught Young Men about Sex," February 1984, 100). But at the same time there are warnings that the relationships between the individual and social convention are difficult and risky. "Those Exhilarating Sex-

ual Sprees" (September 1983, 241) cautions that behavior beyond flirtation is quite risky: "Know yourself. If you're fairly conventional,
prone to guilt feelings, and in the habit of berating yourself for even
small mistakes, you aren't likely to be capable of a joyful spree. Don't
try to force yourself into values—or life styles—that make you uncomfortable" (292). And plenty of *Cosmo*'s short stories show that
adultery is a bad thing for all concerned.

These, then, are *Cosmopolitan's* three genres. What results from
this play within the magazine between bildungsroman, romance, and
novel of manners is an interesting dynamic between the three heroines:
the heroine of the bildungsroman, who is the reader of the magazine;
the heroine of the romance, who is the idealized dream woman;
and the heroine of the novel of manners, who is the much more ordinary woman who must face the way things really are. As she makes
sense of her own psychosexual growth and development, the reader
of the magazine is constantly presented with a choice between her two
sister heroines, the powerful sexy one and her plain sister. Interestingly, the magazine makes a case for and against both ways of being
a woman, with the result that the reader is invited to weigh the arguments and come to her own conclusions. These two types of women
can be represented, for our purposes, by Madonna and Sally Field,
both of whom are interviewed in the same issue of the magazine, although similar alternatives show up in almost every issue. On the one
hand, "Madonna: Inside Me" presents a strong, almost threatening
image of female sexual power. "Crucifixes are sexy because there's a
naked man on them," she tell us, and explains, "I dig skin, lips, and
Latin men. I'm attracted to bums. When I went to Paris, I hung out
with Algerians and Vietnamese guys who didn't have jobs, who just
drove around on motorcycles and terrorized people. I've always been
attracted to people like that" (October 1985, 259). "The Sweet,
Tender Life of Sally Field" (cover title), on the other hand, presents
us with the ordinary woman—not an actress now, but a wife, mother,
and suburban housewife—who has finally found the kind of happiness
her career could never offer. "Not long ago, she and Alan and the two
boys, along with the family dog, Rupert, a gregarious golden retriever,
attended an annual Brentwood parade. 'I stood there watching the
parade pass by—the marching bands and antique cars and the
clowns—surrounded by a crowd of other families, and I felt so terrific
that I almost burst into tears. I felt whole, like I belonged. I now had

a mate, and I was part of the community. I never had this feeling before. I felt a real serenity, like my life was finally on track' " (October 1985, 221). These are not realistic portrayals of complex human beings—judged by such standards, Madonna and Sally Field are impossible cardboard cutouts—but rather female archetypes. This is the angel and the madwoman all over again, or the virgin and the whore, but the magazine can now do something with these two images of female behavior that no other single verbal or visual text can do, precisely because it is a serial publication. Every month or so other versions of these two archetypes appear, and although some issues endorse the madwoman, others endorse the angel, and yet others endorse neither or both. It is impossible to predict before the fact, only to know that the resolution, for any particular month, is unpredictable. One short story, for example, "One of My Best Friends" (October 1985), contrasts the sexy, powerful woman and the "plain Jane also-ran," who are best friends, as they go through courtship and begin careers. Both are quite smart, but while the sexy woman uses her sexuality to succeed in the larger world of business, the plain woman uses her goodness and plainness, mostly, just to find someone to love. The sexy woman becomes a devious trickster, using everyone she can, among them her plain and good friend, for her own selfish purposes, and they become enemies. The plot is convoluted but eventually the sexy woman overreaches, gets into too much trouble, is finally brought down, and the plain woman wins in the end. The message of the fiction is quite clear: Don't be like that woman on the cover of the magazine. Another story takes the other point of view and validates the woman on the cover. "Viable Options" (January 1984) concerns an attractive and successful young career woman who is engaged to the perfect male of her age and class, sweet, gentle, understanding, handsome, but she finds herself drawn to a much older, married, and extremely wealthy Latin male, the head of a successful business, and she struggles to decide between marriage to the one or adultery with the other. She decides in favor of adultery not only because the man has more money and more power and for her, therefore, more sex appeal—but also because the two of them can use their sexual relationship for mutual financial advantage. Because he is the head of a large firm and she is a financial advisor in a position to recommend the stock in his firm to many others, thereby driving up its price, they both stand to gain. Adultery is quite profitable here. Sex and money, the magazine's two turn-ons, are intimately connected and become the "viable options."

This ever-changing story compulsively works over the same ground, sorts through the same evidence, and comes to widely different conclusions. On the central issue, the text is absolutely open. Presented with a similar kind of choice between two extremes in elite literature, Wolfgang Iser (*Implied Reader*) has insisted that the reader has to produce his or her own version, create a third option between the two, rather than accept the ones presented by the text. One can make the same case for *Cosmopolitan* here, at least suggest that when confronted with these two extremes the reader is free to create a third option between them, and certainly, given the text's own widely vacillating attitudes toward these extremes, such a response may be even more likely than that produced by the elite text.

Cosmopolitan and the Woman's Courtship Novel

The way *Cosmopolitan* sets up the dichotomy between sexy ideal and ordinary woman and the way it develops this dichotomy into a more complex text is very much like its own precursor texts, especially *Sense and Sensibility*. It is sense and sensibility in courtship relationships that both Austen's novel and *Cosmopolitan* explore in depth and detail, the problems faced by young women—issues of intimacy, sexuality, and marriage. The parallels between the two texts are worth considering in some detail. *Sense and Sensibility* is concerned with two sisters who are contrasted in precise neoclassical balance—the older, sensible, and rational Elinor versus the younger, emotional, and sensual Marianne—and as they go through a series of comparable courtship experiences the novel evaluates their responses to love and romance. Into this balance Austen introduces one additional way of being a woman, the working-class sexual manipulator, Lucy Steele, who is willing to do whatever is necessary to marry the man with the most money. (She is the precursor of the *Cosmopolitan* cover-story woman.) The plot concerns the pitfalls that face these women: the handsome rake who is only interested in seducing (and then abandoning) them; the amiable oaf who is confused about his own motives and feelings, and so inarticulate that he gives inchoate messages; the older injured male who would father them and is incapable of expressing passion; the older women who would stop them from marrying into their rich and powerful families; the absent mother, or mother surrogate, who deprives them of guidance when they need it most. Austen's novel is praised for the ways in which it raises the issue of sense/sensibility/sexuality, contrasts these opposing character types, and then shows them responding to the assorted men from whom they must choose. These are the issues, characters, and plot devices that appear in *Cosmopolitan*, although the treatment of sexuality is different in at least one major respect: indiscriminate, spontaneous flirtation is the risky behavior of Austen's novel, whereas indiscriminate, spontaneous fornication is the risky behavior of *Cosmopolitan*. This is a difference of the surface only, since the code of manners has changed but remains in place. Thus, for example, to consider for a moment another Austen novel, *Pride and Prejudice*, Elizabeth Bennett learns to tell the difference between her various suitors by the ways in which they dance with her. The reader of *Cosmopolitan* is advised on "What You Can Learn about a Man from His Sexual Style" (June 1989, 172).

Such parallels, of course, do not of themselves make *Cosmopolitan* a great work of literature. Austen's novel is a great work of literature for its depth, the complexity with which it raises and discusses issues; *Cosmopolitan* is at best a cheap and simple version of great art. And yet there is this additional and significant difference between the two texts: The novel unambiguously endorses sense over sensibility and rejects manipulative sexuality outright—Elinor gets the man she wants to marry but Marianne does not, and while Elinor has to put up with some pain silently, Marianne almost dies of grief brought on by the recognition of the emotional abuse to which she has been subjected. Lucy Steele in the background does successfully manipulate herself into marrying the richest, but also the creepiest, man in the novel, and so meets an appropriate fate. The reader is given many challenges by Austen, but no real freedom to evaluate the evidence on her own. It is not possible to decide in favor of Lucy Steele, nor it is possible to decide that Marianne had the better standard of behavior, although a number of readers have argued that Marianne is the more sympathetic, complex, and interesting character. Austen clearly says that Elinor has the better response, directing her reader to the right choice. But *Cosmopolitan* does give the reader the choice. The Austen novel, although more complex in any number of ways—in its use of language, in its insistence on nuance of scene, in the careful way the types can be contrasted with each other—tells the reader what to decide at the end, after leading her through a complex study of the various alternatives. The *Cosmopolitan* text sets the reader free. This is a point of some importance for the study of mass culture, since all of the attacks on mass culture based on the Frankfurt school arguments of the 1930s and 1940s accept Horkheimer and Adorno's analysis that the work of mass culture controls the audience response but the true work of art allows the audience to respond freely. Adorno and Horkheimer and those influenced by them may be right about a number of other mass-cultural texts, but *Cosmopolitan* and *Sense and Sensibility* stand this bit of neo-Marxist orthodoxy on its head.

Cosmopolitan is also a fragmentation and revision of Wharton's *House of Mirth*, the story of the destruction of the strikingly beautiful Lily Bart. In fact, one representative issue of *Cosmopolitan* (December 1988) is a remarkable version of almost all of the major characters, incidents, and concerns of the Wharton novel. Wharton's heroine, living on the edges of wealthy New York society at the turn of the century, has learned to use her beauty as an entrée into a society that values appearances and beautiful things, and although she becomes such a beautiful thing, she is continually compromised because of her beauty, her lack of understanding of money, and her inability to play according to rules of behavior she does not respect, until, losing more and more of her value, she moves down the hierarchy of society and dies poor and alone at the end of the novel of an overdose of a drug designed to give her the energy to work. She does love a sympathetic enough lawyer, but he cannot commit to her or really even understand her, and she turns instead to a series of dull but wealthy men with whom she flirts. She does have a plain but good-hearted friend who tries to support her but is also jealous of and threatened by her. She does consider a proposal of marriage from a Jewish financier, but rejects him because she will not marry down, and later when he is up and she is down, he rejects her because she has become morally compromised. She does try to get a job in a small hat factory and support herself, independent of the world that has rejected her, but she lacks basic job skills and the ability to get along with coworkers. She does have in her possession a series of letters that would compromise her primary female rival and allow her reentry into society, but she refuses to act on feelings of revenge, in good measure because they would also hurt the man she loves.

The December 1988 issue of *Cosmopolitan* includes articles about all of these things. The long piece of fiction in the issue, "The Lap of

Luxury" by William Hamilton, is set in contemporary New York society and concerns a strikingly beautiful woman who has turned herself into a sex/art object in return for the favors of dull, boring, physically repulsive, and financially powerful men. Torn between a poor artist who offers a more authentic relationship and the world of wealth and power, she bungles both and moves down the social scale of New York society. She, too, has a plain friend who tries to be supportive but is also quite jealous of and threatened by her, a woman who emerges at the end as the real heroine. The beautiful woman fails at everything by the end but at least she is not dead—*Cosmopolitan* is, after all, a happier, more upbeat version of the Wharton novel, since Wharton was warning of the dangers of being like Lily Bart, whereas the magazine is willing at least to entertain the possibility that one can be like Lily Bart and survive. She is, of course, on the cover. Above and beyond this story, moreover, there is a surprising number of nonfiction pieces in the issue that repeat *The House of Mirth*. "Marrying Down: Would You Be Up to It?" (212) and "Spotting the Commitment-Shy Man" (124) address two of Lily Bart's primary courtship problems; "Money Talks" (84) discusses the workings of interest in credit card accounts and the value of savings and investments, which Lily did not understand at all. "What Fantasies Can Do for You" (100) urges the reader not to give in to revenge fantasies because they are too dangerous, here repeating Lily's choice; "The Secretarial Job— Still a Great Place to Start" (118) addresses the problems facing a woman in an entry-level job, and "How to Really Succeed on the Job" (220) discusses the problems of getting along with coworkers, situations with which Lily desperately needs help. Then, too, the drug and pep pill advertisements that come near the end of the magazine are the current versions of the drugs that Lily took. And there are other, more minor correlations as well—Lily Bart gets advice from her lawyer friend about the value of collecting Americana in order to use the information to charm one of the men she is courting; the issue of *Cosmopolitan* includes a guide to "The Just-Right Present," which features several pages of photographs of Americana to be given to charm just the right man (194). This is an extraordinary set of parallels, and although it cannot be sustained in every issue of the magazine, it is enough to suggest that a Dadaist anarchist has indeed thrown a hand grenade into the classics. What is perhaps more significant is the message of this issue read against *The House of Mirth*:

Lily did not make a fundamental mistake by turning herself into a work of art and accepting the values of a shallow and materialist society (Wharton's point); she simply lacked the skill to do it well. The point, then, is the way in which the magazine is a rewrite of the classic novel or, to put it another way—since many more people read this issue of the magazine than have ever read *The House of Mirth*—the way readers are being introduced to the situations, characters, and themes of the novel at the present time. The magazine is devoted to producing better Lily Barts and in the process what is lost are the kinds of questions that the novelist can raise. Wharton shows that Lily's desires for love and for money are finally incompatible, that really she must choose, but this issue of *Cosmopolitan* suggests that they are not, that the reader can have both.

And here, finally, it is useful to see the magazine as a fragmentation and revision of *Madame Bovary*, for all of the problems that face Emma Bovary as well—her desire for erotic satisfaction, her larger preoccupations with sensuality, her inability to see men clearly, her lack of knowledge of money and credit, her compulsion to shop, her confused reading habits, even her death—all of these are directly addressed by the magazine. Emma, of course, reads the fashionable women's magazines of her own time and wants an erotically satisfying relationship with a decent man who is capable of loving her for a long time, something her descendants, the readers of *Cosmopolitan*, also want. In Flaubert's version of the story, the woman has no close friends and therefore lacks any trustworthy source of advice and support, but in *Cosmopolitan*'s version, the woman has the magazine itself, created on the model of a close confidant, which supplies her now with all sorts of advice. This best-friend shaping of the magazine appears quite deliberate, since the text begins with the kind of subjects friends might first talk about in initial encounters, books to read, movies to see, music to hear, and then slowly progresses to sharing of secrets and then more intimate advice. (This is, for example, exactly the way Catherine Moreland's friendship with Isabella Thorpe develops in *Northanger Abbey*.) The advice from the magazine functioning as best friend concerns ways of managing money and credit, cautionary tales about women who are sexual addicts, and essays about facing reality, although along with these are also the come-ons from the credit card operations, the advice about how to be more sexual, and the invitations to live the fantasy. Emma was guided by her reading of the romantic fantasies of her adolescence; *Cosmopolitan* prods the reader to see the complexity and diversity of the choices she must make between fantasy and reality, and while she can be guided by the fantasy and choose like Emma, she can also be guided by the more realistic content, or by bits and pieces of both. She has more options than Emma, even if the choices between fantasy and reality are not given equal weight. The novel, furthermore, offers no convincing explanation of why Emma must reject her fantasies, except of course for the demonstration that sensual pleasures are inherently destructive for Flaubert, but the magazine offers the modern reader the opportunity to accept sensual pleasures without dying, and to understand that the fantasy can be workable or unworkable, depending on the strengths and desires of the individual woman. In Flaubert's version of the story, the woman does not understand men and is devastated as each relationship ends, and although she learns something from each failure, it is never enough. She cannot master intimacy. In *Cosmopolitan*'s version of the story the woman may not understand men and may have just as many failed relationships, but except in some of the most despairing letters to Irma Kurtz, she is always ready to try again, and most of the time she appears to have the ability to learn from her mistakes. In "An Affair to Remember: What It Was Like to Live with and Be Loved by Cary Grant" (June 1989, 180), for example, the author plays Emma to Grant's Rudolphe, and is finally able to walk away from the seductive male when she discovers the reality behind the fantasy—he wears women's underwear, is incapable of real love, and is an overbearing and controlling father. "Diana Ross and the Men in Her Life" (November 1989, 280) follows Ross through a number of failed relationships until she succeeds in one at last, and "Candice Bergen: Beauty with a Cutting Edge" (November 1989, 222) does the same with Bergen. These women do master intimacy. Emma dies, whereas the modern reader learns about people like Emma, some of whom prosper and some of whom die, and thereby has a better chance of choosing what is best for herself. The price she pays, the subscription to the magazine, is the rather ingenious capitalistic solution to the problems that destroy Emma, for L'Heureux's successor has found a way to make even more money than L'Heureux himself. The merchant/usurer lost a good customer when Emma died; his successor knows enough to keep the customer satisfied.

The pattern of correspondences between the magazine and the great courtship novels of the age of realism is extensive, intricate, and important. Writers such as Austen, Flaubert, and Wharton, who were addressing in their times almost exactly the same issues that *Cosmopolitan* addresses today, created stories that are almost exactly like those that *Cosmopolitan* is creating today. All of them, individual authors and corporate collective alike, were responding to what they believed were the needs of their readers, and quite clearly those needs have not changed very much. *Sense and Sensibility, The House of Mirth*, and *Madame Bovary* are novels that are also cautionary tales and guides for young women readers; *Cosmopolitan* is a cautionary tale and a guide for young women readers that is also a novel. They meet on the middle ground.

Certain things are lost in the *Cosmopolitan* version, of course: the rich verbal texture of the novels, the play of small detail, the complex description of place, the elaboration of motive. The magazine is written in a much more limited, even impoverished language, and yet it does offer us something in return, the rich visual texture of the advertisements and illustrations. Flaubert describes wedding feast and landscape; *Cosmopolitan* presents vivid images arranged behind wedding dresses, perfume bottles, and breasts. To note the poverty of verbal texture in *Cosmopolitan* is to explain only half of the nature of this new text.

And the magazine does something more, at least in some of its fiction: Like other works praised by literary critics, it can be self-reflexive, turning back on itself to question its own function. One piece of fiction will serve to demonstrate, "Facemaker" (March 1988), which concerns a reporter for a "glitzy women's magazine" who is injured and requires plastic surgery. She finds the best man in the business, "an artist, a sculptor with flesh and bone, someone who could create an entirely new person with a gilt-edge future," but it soon becomes clear that this surgeon has been "duplicating women" and "mass-producing faces" by creating the same face on every woman in the course of trying to create the perfect woman's face, the one that belongs on the cover of women's magazines (that point is explicitly noted). As it happens, each time he muffs up in some little way, and, perfectionist that he is, to cover up he kills the woman, cutting off her head and keeping it in his office. When the heroine discovers all this she turns for help to her editor, a man "educated at Berkeley, troubled by the decline of liberalism in the mid-eighties," who "cared more about those who couldn't afford his magazine and the products it advertised" and who "often spent holidays working in soup kitchens." With his help the heroine is able to kill the surgeon just in the nick of time, and then she notes, as the story ends, in an altogether different tone, that "her face was his gift, and it was—as he had dreamed—a magnificent face. He had given her hope. He had given her a future" (298). It's all here: the glitzy magazine, the face of the cover, the guilt, the mass production of identical faces, the identification of that kind of mass production with mutilation, the decapitation of real women, and their death, even the pleasure at the end that the face itself has its compensations.

PART 3

History

Only a historical view provides a perspective from which to assess the richness and poverty of the contemporary, to see what has been gained from this break with the past and what has been lost—and might be regained.

Gerald Graff, *Literature against Itself* (1979)

CHAPTER 11

STAR TREK, GULLIVER'S TRAVELS,
and the Problem of History

Some stories are about history. *Star Trek*, for example, owes much of its considerable success to its ability to tell us compelling allegories about our own history, everything from the war in Vietnam and the fall of the Soviet empire to the international drug trade and the continuing conflicts between Arabs and Jews, all of which it displaces into a fanciful high-tech world of the twenty-third and twenty-fourth centuries. Although the program explains the present by disguising it as the future, as a contemporary variant on *Gulliver's Travels*, Jonathan Swift's satiric allegory about human nature first published in 1726, *Star Trek* does this by turning systematically to the past. The problem of history is not simple.

To hold *Star Trek* up to *Gulliver's Travels* is to see just how closely Gene Roddenberry replicates Swift's model. The various *Star Trek* casts travel to an assortment of exotic and fanciful worlds where they meet superpowerful and superweak aliens, misguided scientists, talking creatures, and apelike humanoids, just as Gulliver travels to an assortment of exotic and fanciful islands where he meets tiny people, powerful giants, misguided scientists, talking horses, and apelike humanoids. The strange new worlds that *Star Trek* comes upon are thinly veiled allegories about life in contemporary America, those that Gulliver comes upon, about life in eighteenth-century England. The various *Star Trek* crews discover political incompetence, military adventurism, and personal selfishness as well as some well-meaning attempts at utopia, and Gulliver discovers much the same. Spock, one of *Star Trek*'s most endearing creations, is constantly torn between logic and emotion, just as Gulliver finds himself positioned between creatures who live according to reason and emotion in his last and most interesting voyage.

There is, however, a significant shift in point of view, and it is here that our own history can be seen most clearly. In place of Swift's strong belief in individual self-reliance, the *Star Trek* stories stress teamwork and cooperation; in place of his criticism of English nationalism and European colonialism, *Star Trek* celebrates America's strong presence in the universe; in place of his hostility toward science, *Star Trek* celebrates the benefits of technology; and in place of his love of the past and denigration of the future, *Star Trek* substitutes its denigration of the past and love of the future. Whatever works out badly in Swift—and there is much to be depressed about—usually works out quite well in *Star Trek*. But although *Star Trek* may seem like *Gulliver's Travels* as seen through rose-colored glasses, it should also be recognized as the successful resolution of the problems Swift posed so eloquently in his story for which he could find no helpful answers. The irreconcilable oppositions in *Gulliver's Travels*, which are the root cause of so much of his despair—oppositions between individual and society, reason and emotion, common sense and technology, human and alien—are consistently (and often triumphantly) reconciled by *Star Trek*. And although Swift might not have been pleased by the result, many intelligent Americans are devoted fans. There may be many reasons for this but one certainly is that *Star Trek* changes *Gulliver's Travels* so that it fits much more closely with contemporary American realities. What William Whyte described as the social ethic of American society more than a generation ago in *The Organization Man*, "a belief in the group as the source of creativity; a belief in 'belongingness' as the ultimate need of the individual; and a belief in the application of science to achieve the belongingness" (7), is the ethic of our own version of *Gulliver's Travels*, along with a different attitude toward the burdens of empire.

Star Trek is *Gulliver's Travels* for the American empire. The various captains of the various *Enterprise*s proudly remind us at the beginning of each episode that their mission is to explore strange new worlds and "to boldly go" where no one has gone before. Gulliver has been there before, of course, only much less boldly, either shipwrecked or abandoned by his mates, never having sought contact with alien life forms in the first place. The various *Star Trek* crews have a great many more weapons than Gulliver, and a great many more reasons to use them: Gulliver is typically a captive in the new place, at the mercy of natives who don't know what to make of him, but as standard bearers of the United Federation of Planets the *Star Trek* crews are powerful outsiders, involved in complex battles with the natives of the place or with other evil forces in space. They are the police. Gulliver must ingratiate himself as best he can with his captors, pleading for his liberty and for their protection and kindness, for there is no other way he can survive. *Star Trek* operates from strength rather than weakness.

Star Trek and *Gulliver's Travels* are stories about two very different stages in the history of exploration and conquest. Driven by wanderlust and, as a merchant seaman, by the desire for personal profit, Gulliver voyages to dangerous and unexplored areas of the planet; although the crews of the *Enterprise* also voyage to the dangerous and often unexplored areas of the universe, it is now to enforce governmental regulations that require peace and stability everywhere. Their awkward interference in the internal affairs of the peoples they come upon replaces Gulliver's customary habit of observation and education. To be fair to *Star Trek*, the universe it explores is full of dangerous and deranged egomaniacs, out-of-control spaceships and space probes that are able to drain energy from everything in their path, and whole races of dangerous villains such as the Klingons. The fact that the *Enterprise* does get involved in battles seems natural enough. And yet Gulliver meets a whole race of tiny men who plot to put out his eyes and then starve him to death, giant insects and rodents that try to destroy him, and an impressive array of lunatic scientists and revoltingly ugly human beings from which he must keep a safe distance. He, too, must fight to survive, and is especially proud of the way he is able to carve up the giant rodents and dispatch the giant insects. But these battles are never foregrounded as they are in *Star Trek*, and Gulliver is able to concentrate on other matters, particularly on the habits and customs of the alien cultures. This type of observation is rarely of much interest to the crews of the *Enterprise*, except to the extent that it can help them out of a tight jam. When Gulliver stumbles upon a strange new world, he must struggle to eat yet another local diet and learn yet another language, but when the crew of the *Enterprise* stumbles upon a strange new world, not only do they usually carry their own food supply, but almost all of the aliens they meet speak perfect English, and in those rare cases when they do not, the *Enterprise* has translators and decoders that do the work instantaneously.

Because this is now a story that typically supports America's sense of its mission in the world whereas Swift's story constantly questions England's sense of its mission, *Star Trek*'s optimism and confidence replace Gulliver's bitter misanthropy. Indeed, the very existence of these technologically advanced space travelers in the twenty-third century proves that things are getting better, since all manner of wonderful improvements have taken place since the primitive days of the twentieth century. The opposite is the case in *Gulliver's Travels*. Gulliver is an extremely patriotic Englishman, very proud of his country's customs and accomplishments, but in the context of his travels Swift makes Gulliver's patriotism seem absurd and foolish, and Gulliver himself finally comes to the same conclusion. The *Star Trek* crews are extremely patriotic earthlings, very proud of the United Federation of Planets' customs and accomplishments, and sometimes unconsciously smug about being human. In the context of their adventures, the program's writers make this out to be a very fine thing, indeed. No race in *Star Trek* ever approaches the grand accomplishments of the human beings. Swift doubtless would have gagged, but he might have been impressed by the extent to which *Star Trek* revises his story. Each of Gulliver's four voyages has reappeared one or more times as the basis for a *Star Trek* movie or television program.

Voyage One: Lilliput and Vietnam

An episode from the original *Star Trek* television series, "A Private Little War," produced in 1968 at the height of the Vietnam War, is extremely similar to Gulliver's first voyage to Lilliput. A dark and despairing assessment of American foreign policy, it is also evidence that not all *Star Trek* stories have hopeful or upbeat endings. Kirk and his colleagues visit a primitive planet that is divided between their friends, the peaceful hill people, and mean hippie-like villagers who are secretly being armed with advanced flintlock rifles by the Klingons, the Soviet-like enemies of the United Federation of Planets. The leader of the hill people is a pacifist, but he is married to a racially exotic female witch doctor who demands that Captain Kirk supply them with fancy new weapons after she saves his life. Kirk reluctantly agrees, but there is immediate trouble. When the leader refuses to fire his new flintlock rifle, his wife steals Kirk's powerful phaser weapon and runs off to join the other side. The other side first tries to rape her and then kills her, and Kirk's old pacifist friend decides he must become a fighter. As the program ends, Kirk arms the rest of the hill people, although not without a great deal of soul searching and angst.

This is Gulliver's voyage to Lilliput turned into a story about Vietnam. Gulliver comes upon a society of tiny men and women whose religion and politics mimic the customs of Swift's England, and quickly becomes involved in its long-standing war with its equally tiny neighbor state, Blefuscu, which represents France. Although Gulliver at first takes up the battle on behalf of Lilliput, after destroying the enemy's fleet he realizes the tyrannical designs of the Lilliputian emperor and refuses further service. The Lilliputians plot to blind and starve him to death for this and other affronts to their pride, but he is able to escape and make his way back home. Both "A Private Little War" and the voyage to Lilliput involve a strong and powerful voyager who visits a world of much weaker people who suffer from pettiness, distrust, and treachery. In each story a conflict quickly develops between the voyager and the people he meets who wish to involve him in a war in progress. Cooperating at first, the voyager faces greater and greater demands on his power and strength and soon understands that he will never be able to resolve the conflict to his satisfaction. For Gulliver the solution is relatively simple: caught in an allegory about the eighteenth-century wars between England and France, he flees for his life. For Kirk the solution is not simple at all: caught in an allegory of the Vietnam War, he cannot escape, but becomes instead the reluctant arms supplier to allies that he admits he is destroying, both physically and spiritually. Both Kirk and Gulliver attempt to maintain the balance of power, Kirk by intervening on behalf of the hill people, Gulliver by refusing to intervene on behalf of the Lilliputians. The ends are the same but the means are different. Both stories are also concerned with the issue of freedom. Gulliver draws the line where his behavior would conflict with principles of freedom, refusing to help the Lilliputians turn their opponents into slaves; by contrast, Kirk gives weapons to the hill people so that they might preserve their freedom, regardless of the consequences to their way of life. In both stories, the innocent are corrupted—Kirk's pacifist friends in "A Private

Little War," Gulliver himself in the voyage to Lilliput when he is drawn briefly into the combat. And here, too, is another significant difference: Gulliver remains relatively innocent through it all, but Kirk and his colleagues are forced to deal with complex situations that defy easy answers; perhaps they do not act as wisely as Gulliver, who learns not to interfere, but they do act with an awareness of the moral quagmire in which they find themselves. The clear good and evil of Swift's moral and political vision is replaced here by a much more muddled and confused reality in which all alternatives are bad.

Voyage Two: Redeeming Swift

"You've saved humanity once again," the superbeing Q tells Captain Picard at the end of the final episode of the *Star Trek: The Next Generation* television series. Produced in 1994, "All Good Things" is the story of the *Enterprise*'s helplessness before the Q Continuum, an immensely powerful entity that holds human beings in great contempt; it is also a much more upbeat variation on Gulliver's second voyage, to Brobdingnag. A representative of this world, the character known as Q, appears on board the *Enterprise* and puts Picard on trial for being a member of a "dangerous, savage, child race." He has done this once before in the very first episode of the series, "Encounter at Far Point Station," produced in 1987, when Picard successfully demonstrated that human beings had become "peaceful and beneficial." But now Q tells Picard that the original trial has never ended and that he has become deeply disappointed with Picard and his crew since that encounter. Picard is once more on trial, and if he fails all human life will be destroyed. The particular problem Q designs for Picard involves all sorts of confusing distortions in space and time, but it ultimately depends on the captain's skill in learning not to fight. Although Picard's first impulse is to order the *Enterprise* to shoot at a potential enemy, perceived simultaneously in the past, the present, and the future, he finally understands that this weapon fire is growing into a cosmic firestorm that will prevent the creation of life on earth if it cannot be stopped. When Picard orders all the *Enterprise*s to stop firing in the past, the present, and the future, he saves mankind. It is a neat little parable, and a story that once again echoes Swift.

Gulliver's voyage to Brobdingnag takes him to a land of giant-sized humans who have evolved into a peaceable, just, and decent society, and although the Brobdingnagians are still subject to human passions and sometimes slip from the ideal, they are consistently more decent and civilized than Gulliver's own countrymen. Indeed, the Brobding-nagian king tells Gulliver that the Europeans he praises so highly and describes so honestly are "the most pernicious race of little odious vermin that Nature ever suffered to crawl upon the surface of the earth" (II, 6, p. 173), and although Gulliver is at first greatly offended, he gradually comes to see the truth of this position. Q's contempt for Picard's race is similar to the king's contempt for Gulliver's. But Q is at once more savage and more compassionate: the king merely con-demns Gulliver's kind, but Q acts, setting up a test for Picard that will result in either the destruction or the redemption of human beings. Gulliver is weak and unimportant in comparison to the Brobdingna-gian giants, and although he does defend himself from small animals, essentially his destiny is out of his control. There is nothing he can do to change the king's opinion. Picard is also weak and unimportant in comparison to the Q Continuum, but Q puts him in an important position and requires that he act. His destiny is in his control. When Picard passes the test and redeems life at the end of the story, Q seems more than a little pleased and Picard thanks him for his help. It turns out that Q does not really hate human beings after all; he is really more like the Brobdingnagians' king than he first appears.

The problem Picard solves in the story is one of the central issues raised by Swift in the Brobdingnag voyage. Gulliver offers the king the formula for making gunpowder so that he can experience the glo-ries of blowing up buildings, ships, and people and thereby appreciate European technology. The king is horrified and forbids Gulliver to speak about the subject again, but in his encounter with Q Picard learns how to discard fighting as an option, moving beyond what Swift was willing to imagine. "All Good Things" is more hopeful than the Brobdingnag voyage, but it makes a very similar statement. In one story human beings are pernicious vermin because they love war, and in the other human beings are pernicious vermin because they love war and if they don't learn to stop fighting they will be destroyed. I wrote my book, Gulliver says in his introductory letter, so that my readers would see their vices and correct them, but I despair that any-one will do it. Picard corrects his vices.

If Picard can be seen as Gulliver's perfect reader, the one he could not find in 1726, Q himself seems more than a little like Swift. Alternately mocking and contemptuous, Q's moods are Swift's. At one moment he is making fun of the follies of the human race and at another savagely denouncing their vices, with warmth and affection hidden within. Capable of moving back and forth in history, Q appears on "Encounter at Far Point Station" dressed first as an eighteenth-century pirate, then as a twentieth-century American soldier, then as a twenty-first-century armored warrior—there is a certain theatrical campiness about his performance—as he acts out a history of the human race that Swift would absolutely endorse. When Picard stands up to Q and says that he does not want to be judged by the past, essentially by Swift's perspective, Q gives him a chance to show that humans have improved. And in both the first and last episodes, Picard demonstrates that. We are, these programs insist, beyond Swift.

Voyage Three: San Francisco and Laputa

Star Trek IV: The Voyage Home (1987) is a similarly upbeat variation on Gulliver's third voyage to Laputa and its neighboring islands. In this movie, a space probe of unknown origin and immense power approaches the earth, creating torrential rain storms, blocking out the sun, and draining all energy supplies. Kirk and his crew, returning from the planet Vulcan on a captured Klingon ship, are warned away from what looks like the end of the world. But Kirk vows to save civilization and Spock figures out that the probe is trying to make contact with humpback whales, long extinct on twenty-third-century earth. The crew does the sensible thing and time travels back to twentieth-century San Francisco in order to retrieve some whales, but this is a tricky business that involves swinging the battered Klingon ship around the sun. They succeed, of course, but their mishaps in what Kirk calls the "primitive and paranoid culture" of the late twentieth century are some of *Star Trek*'s most Swiftian jabs at human nature. The city that they enter is polluted, filled with homicidal taxi drivers, loud noise, indifferent pedestrians, crooked pawn shop owners, hostile policemen, angry garbage men, and incredibly antisocial punks who play loud music from ghetto blasters on the city's bus lines. "It's a miracle these people ever got out of the twentieth century," Dr. McCoy remarks.

The key elements in this movie—the threat from a probe that blocks out the sun, the ability to time travel, the attack on foolish behavior, and the promise of technology—are all key elements in Gulliver's third voyage. The probe in *The Voyage Home* is a kinder and gentler version of Swift's floating island of Laputa, which hovers over the larger land mass of Balnibarbi. A king lives on Laputa but controls his subjects who live on the land below by moving his floating island over their cities and depriving them of sun and rain, pelting them with rocks, and letting "the island drop directly upon their heads." The probe in *The Voyage Home* is similarly destructive, but without the malice and intent of the Laputian king. Kirk and his crew find a way to get rid of the probe, but the best that the inhabitants of Balnibarbi can do is to erect towers to keep the island from crashing down on their heads. Laputa remains in the sky, capable of wreaking havoc on their civilization. What can't be solved in *Gulliver's Travels* can in *The Voyage Home*.

In a similar fashion, time travel in *The Voyage Home* is much more positive and upbeat than it is in Swift. On Glubbdubdrib, another island on this third voyage, Gulliver finds magicians who can recall people from the dead, and with their assistance he sees a number of figures from ancient and modern history. While all of the ancients are noble and virtuous, the moderns are degenerate whores, cowards, and fools, and Gulliver is discouraged to see just how horribly the human race has degenerated (although he has learned this same lesson in his voyage to Brobdingnag). In *The Voyage Home* it is the twentieth-century ancients who are stupid, selfish, and criminal and the twenty-third-century moderns who are noble and the virtuous. Kirk and his crew may be irritated by the past, but they are immensely encouraged to see just how gloriously the human race has evolved.

In its attacks on twentieth-century civilization, *The Voyage Home* comes closest to Swift's satire, although even here it is somewhat less savage. The San Francisco that Kirk and his crew visit may be a place of venal stupidity, but it is not quite as bad as the places Gulliver visits, the Laputians who are lost in abstract (and meaningless) thought, the Balibarbians who turn fertile lands into wastelands, the Struldbruggs who turn the promise of eternal life into misery.

Science and technology, which are forces for good in *The Voyage Home*, are forces for harm in *Gulliver's Travels*. In the Academy at Lagado, Gulliver sees experiments to extract sunbeams from cucumbers, to turn excrement into food, and to breed wool-less sheep. But it is *Star Trek*'s medical technology that comes to the rescue in *The Voyage Home*, and the long history of technological progress in *Star Trek* that allows the crew to time travel and save humanity. Technology is the great seductive promise in *Star Trek*, the great seductive catastrophe in Swift. When Kirk's crew offers a twentieth-century engineer the formula for transparent aluminum, the engineer's eyes light up with glee, while McCoy whispers diabolically that the formula will bring him wealth beyond his wildest dreams. The technology is passed on. In the comparable moment in Swift, Gulliver offers the king of Brobdingnag the formula for gunpowder, but the king is appalled. The technology is not passed on.

Voyage Three Again: Dutch Traders and Ferengi

Gulliver's third voyage begins when his ship is overpowered by Japanese pirates led by a Dutchman who has a virulent hatred for Christians, and it ends when his ship is intercepted by Dutch traders who demand that he trample on a crucifix. Although these interactions are short, they show that Swift believed that the ethic of the Dutch people, the most successful commercial trading nation of his time, was incompatible with Christianity, and that traders were only slightly more civilized than pirates. The Ferengi are *Star Trek*'s Dutch traders, a race like the Yankee traders of eighteenth- and nineteenth-century earth history, we learn in "The Last Outpost" episode of *The Next Generation* (1987), where *Star Trek* meets these "mercantile and territorial opportunists . . . with the worst qualities of capitalists" for the first time. Although the Ferengi are every bit as repulsive as Swift's pirate traders, Picard and his crew understand that they must be given a chance to redeem themselves. When the *Enterprise* and the Ferengi ship are each rendered powerless as they pass a lifeless planet, the respective crews are forced to cooperate on the planet's surface in order to determine what is going on. Jabbering and jumping around like monkeys, the Ferengi double-cross the *Enterprise* crew and, as they fight back, an automated figure from an ancient civilization materializes in front of them and tries to evaluate the claims of the two sides. This godlike figure is so impressed by *Star Trek*'s wisdom—that skill in fighting means knowing when not to fight—that he sides with the *Enterprise*. This figure is willing to kill all the Ferengis on the spot, but *Star Trek* asks that they be allowed to live, since they deserve the chance to develop and learn. Would Gulliver have been so charitable? It is hard to say, since the situation does not arise, but if Gulliver detests the Dutch because they are so unchristian, the *Enterprise* crew demonstrates true Christian charity. These are positive and negative versions of the same basic story.

Voyage Four: Houyhnhnms, Yahoos, and Spock

Contained in bits and pieces throughout the original *Star Trek* television series and movies is the ongoing saga of Spock, the half-human/half-Vulcan who lives out the conflicts between his emotional and rational inheritances. Always more comfortable with logic, Spock nevertheless moves awkwardly into emotional life and he is always better for it when he does. As Spock puts it in *The Undiscovered Country*, "Logic is the beginning of wisdom, not the end." Spock dies at the end of *Star Trek II: The Wrath of Khan* in order to save his fellow crew members because "the needs of the many outweigh the needs of the few, or the one." Reborn in *Star Trek III: The Search for Spock* when his friends disregard orders and rescue his immature body from a disintegrating planet, he grows quickly to adulthood but without any knowledge of his prior life. Back on the planet Vulcan he is retrained in all the logical arts, but although he quickly masters Vulcan knowledge, when the computer asks him, "How do you feel?" he does not understand the question. His human mother standing nearby asks him "if the good of the many outweighs the good of the one," and when he replies that it does, she tells him, "You stand here alive because of a mistake made by your flawed, feeling, human friends. They have sacrificed their futures because they believed that the good of the one, you, was more important to them." "Humans make illogical decisions," Spock says. "They do indeed," she answers. But by the end of the film Spock has relearned feeling, and it is that intuitive, irrational skill that enables him to save the crew once again when he must guess at the complex math computations that allow them to time travel into the twentieth century. His message to his mother at the very end of the movie, which is to be conveyed through his logical Vulcan father, is "I feel fine." This is a moment of victory, of the balance regained between reason and emotion.

And it is in stark contrast to the predicament of Gulliver, whose fourth voyage takes him to the country of the Houyhnhnms, where calm and intelligent horses live as masters in a perfectly rational society and where the only danger comes from the dung-throwing, filthy, and completely emotional Yahoos, humans who have degenerated to the most odious of life forms. Gulliver is caught in the same emotional/rational split that Spock balances so gloriously, but in the land of the Houyhnhnms he makes a very different choice than Spock does. Houyhnhnms are almost exactly like Vulcans—gently affectionate to all, incapable of telling an untruth, rational to an extreme—but Yahoos are exaggeratedly repulsive versions of humans, and Gulliver rejects them. Swift presents Gulliver with a skewed set of alternatives, and so he renounces his biological ties to the Yahoos and tries to make himself as much as possible like a Houyhnhnm. But when a young Yahoo female tries to rape him, the Houyhnhmns understand that he is a Yahoo and order him to leave their island, fearing that he could lead a rebellion of the Yahoos against them. Gulliver is crushed and returns to England a complete misanthrope, barely able to stand the sight, let alone the smell, of his own human family. Gulliver is definitely not fine at the end of his last voyage and has serious psychological problems—this is where his rejection of his emotional Yahoo heritage has led him. By contrast, Spock, who has learned emotions without ever rejecting logic, is gloriously alive and healthy.

Swift and Roddenberry tell the same basic story about the importance of finding a balance between reason and emotion, one using a negative example and the other a positive one. Gulliver admires the fact that the Houyhnhnms cannot lie, and although Spock explains that he cannot lie, when he learns to stretch the truth a bit it is a victory both for him and for his human companions. Gulliver embraces the rational ideal; several centuries later, Kirk and his friends must gently pull Spock away from the limitations of such an ideal, back to the values of irrational human behavior. In a place like Lilliput the good of the many clearly outweighs the good of the one. In *Star Trek* the good of the many outweighs the good of the one, and then the opposite is affirmed as well, the good of the one outweighs the good of the many. Nothing much is in balance in Gulliver's various travels. Everything can be brought into balance in *Star Trek*, where the individual and the group take turns supporting each other. This is a profound improvement in the conditions of existence.

The predicament of Gulliver at the end of the fourth voyage, when he wishes to renounce his own savage species and join the much gentler Houyhnhmns but is sent away, is the subject of a 1994 story from *Deep Space Nine* about a teenage boy named Rugal. Biologically Rugal is a Cardassian, a nasty, warlike race of humanoids who have heads that resemble oversized baseballs to which spoons have been attached upside-down above their noses. (American sports heroes with cocaine habits?) Rugal wants to become a Bajoran, the gentle pastoral race of humanoids with ridges on their noses who have suffered for many years under a horrible military occupation by the Cardassians. Abandoned by the Cardassians when they left Bajor, Rugal has been adopted by a Bajoran and has begun to learn his gentle ways. He hates Cardassians and knows that they killed millions of innocent Bajorians during the occupation. Now, however, a belligerent Cardassian military commander demands that he be turned over to his father, and Commander Sisko has the task of deciding what to do. What he learns is that Rugal is a pawn in a complex Cardassian military scheme to humiliate Rugal's father, a Cardassian politician who opposes military rule. If he can be shown to have lost his son, he will no longer be a threat. Sisko therefore determines that Rugal must go back to Cardassia. Rugal is in the same predicament as Gulliver here, for if he stays with the gentle species, he will inadvertently give power to the evil species. Gulliver is horrified at his destiny, but Rugal appears reconciled to his. What works out badly in *Gulliver's Travels* works out well in *Star Trek*.

But the much longer Cardassia and Bajor story line, to which this Rugal episode belongs, is full of ongoing treacheries that are not so simply or happily resolved. Because the militaristic Cardassians have occupied pastoral Bajor, killed many of its inhabitants, and then left many of the children they fathered behind, the story seems at times to be an allegory of the U.S. involvement in Vietnam. Just as Gulliver, the representative Englishman, comes upon a new world that is England all over again, Sisko and the *Deep Space Nine* crew, the representative Americans, come upon Cardassia, which is America all over again. Swift uses the technique to trash England; the writers of this *Deep Space Nine* story use the technique to trash America. This is no longer an upbeat and rose-colored version of *Gulliver's Travels*—but it is also an unusual story line for *Star Trek*.

Gulliver's Travels occupies a privileged position in the history of our literature. Enshrined in the canon of great books taught by our colleges and universities, it is praised as one of the greatest and most sustained satires ever written in the English language—which is to say that it is extremely critical of human nature. This is missing from most of *Star Trek*, but all the rest of Swift's material remains: the inquiry into the nature of civilization, the use of allegory, the elaboration of the fantastic voyage, the problem of reason and emotion. In two more centuries, the students at whatever will replace our colleges and universities may be studying *Star Trek* with the same care and intensity we lavish on *Gulliver's Travels*.

CHAPTER 12

The Great Books in Vietnam

When it was finally over we made sense of the war in Vietnam through a series of popular movies. Although they were obviously meant to explain recent American history, all of the major films in this group are contemporary variants on the great war or warrior stories of the past. The surface details evoke Vietnam, showing My Lai–type massacres, disabled veterans in decrepit VA hospitals, and POWs held in makeshift jungle prisons, but the fundamental plot lines, character types, and thematic preoccupations upon which these details depend for their coherence and larger meanings come straight out of Homer and Aristophanes, Spenser and Shakespeare, Cooper, Conrad, and Remarque. American film audiences have come to understand what we did in Vietnam almost exclusively in terms of the great tradition of literature, having seen some of the very worst moments of our history shaped according to what Matthew Arnold ("Culture and Anarchy") once called the best that had been thought and said in culture. At a time when critics have been warning us about the death or irrelevance of serious literature, the battle for our hearts and minds has been fought using the great books of Western civilization. It has involved the participants in a series of fiercely partisan revisions, as filmmakers have turned to the classics in order to respond to and correct each other's works, something they have often done in great and meticulous detail. Homer has been used as ammunition against Conrad, Conrad as a weapon against Cooper,

and Spenser as a force to oppose all three in a literary free-for-all with
very high political stakes: understanding Vietnam.

Although Francis Ford Coppola made it clear at the time that *Apocalypse Now* (1979) was based on Joseph Conrad's *Heart of Darkness*,
and Michael Cimino's *Deer Hunter* (1978) invites obvious comparison with James Fenimore Cooper's *Deerslayer*, the classical back-
grounds of the other films in this group have not been as easy for us
to see. And yet they are just as important. Hal Ashby's *Coming Home*
(1978) and Sylvester Stallone's *First Blood* (1982) repeat the characters and plots of *The Odyssey*, Homer's epic poem about the return
of Odysseus after the war in Troy, and Stallone's sequel, *Rambo: First
Blood, Part II* (1985), is a careful and extensive retelling of *The Iliad*,
Homer's epic poem about the anger of Achilles during the war in Troy.
Oliver Stone's *Platoon* (1986) takes over the basic content of Shakespeare's history play about Falstaff and Hotspur, *Henry IV, Part I*,
while Stanley Kubrick's *Full Metal Jacket* (1987) repeats key elements
of Louis Milestone's 1930 Hollywood movie version of Erich Maria
Remarque's antiwar novel *All Quiet on the Western Front*. Barry Levinson's *Good Morning, Vietnam* (1988) is very similar to *The Acharnians*, Aristophanes' antiwar comedy about one man's attempt to
make peace with the enemy. And Oliver Stone's film version of Ron
Kovic's life story, *Born on the Fourth of July* (1989), is yet another
variation on Homer's *Odyssey*. To this list of major films about Vietnam must be added George Lucas's *Star Wars* trilogy, since the second
and third films in the series, *The Empire Strikes Back* (1980) and *The
Return of the Jedi* (1983), are filled with obvious references to Vietnam, where primitive jungle people defend their homeland against the
attack of an advanced technological empire. Lucas explained that he
modeled the evil emperor on Richard Nixon. And the *Star Wars* trilogy, as I have argued at the beginning of this book, is an elegant
adaptation of Edmund Spenser's great Renaissance epic about sol-
diering, *The Faerie Queene*.

There are only so many experiences that a soldier can have during
and after a war, of course, but although this may explain some of the
similarities between these movies and great books of the past, the
correlations between them are so extensive and specific that something
else must be at work here. For most of the movies in this group at
least there seems no other possible conclusion but that filmmakers
have consistently relied on the great books to give form and meaning

to the Vietnam experience. We have turned to Homer, Shakespeare, and their peers in order to figure out what we did in Vietnam and what it all means. But is this right? Can the stories that Homer tells us about the events of the Trojan War help explain our behavior in Vietnam more than three thousand years later? Can Shakespeare's story of civil war in England be transplanted to Vietnam and still be meaningful, not as a production of Shakespeare in modern dress, but as an Oliver Stone movie that purports to speak truthfully about his experiences in Vietnam? Vietnam is not ancient Troy or Renaissance England, and the wisdom of the great books of the past should not be able to explain present conditions so accurately and precisely. And yet the evidence from these movies suggests that in this crucial period, Homer, Shakespeare, and a handful of other major writers became the dominant voices in our debate over the meaning of Vietnam, although they were writing imaginative stories about other wars in other times and places. Great literature, critics are fond of saying, endures because it can be constantly reinterpreted, and this is what our filmmakers have been doing here, often with brilliant results.

But even if these films manage to evade the actual history of the war in Vietnam, because they engage each other in sustained arguments over the meaning of that war they create their own film history. Conservative and liberal versions of the great books of the past alternate with each other in a series of politically charged debates over the central issues of the war and, ultimately, the meanings of the great books themselves. A liberal's version of *The Odyssey, Coming Home*, is answered by a conservative's version, *First Blood*, in an argument about the problems faced by the returning Vietnam veteran and the correct interpretation of Homer's poem. The conservative's straightforward and unambiguous story about the white man and the savage, *The Deer Hunter*, is answered by the liberal's deeply ambiguous and troubled version of the same, *Apocalypse Now*, in an argument over guilt and responsibility in Vietnam and the conflicting moral visions of James Fenimore Cooper and Joseph Conrad. The liberal's celebration of the epic achievement of American rebels and their Vietnamese allies in the *Star Wars* trilogy is answered by the conservative's celebration of the epic achievement of an American soldier in *Rambo: First Blood, Part II*. The argument is over the nature of heroic behavior in Vietnam and the conflicting value systems of Spenser and Homer. A soldier like Han Solo meets a soldier like Rambo in *Platoon*, a movie that takes this ongoing conflict between conservative and liberal versions of the war as the subject of its story, but Oliver Stone's movie is also an interpretation of Shakespeare's version of the same kind of conflict. After *Platoon,* as the debate shifts to issues within the antiwar Left, the tragicomic antiwar movie *Full Metal Jacket,* which shows the weakness of the comic attitude toward war, is answered by the tragicomic antiwar movie *Good Morning, Vietnam,* which shows the strength of the comic attitude. *Full Metal Jacket* shows the process by which all recruits are turned into killers, even the peace-loving liberals; *Good Morning, Vietnam* shows how one peace-loving liberal heroically resists the transformation. The argument is over the power of an individual soldier to maintain integrity, decency, and humanity and over the conflicting ideas of Remarque and Aristophanes, on whose works these particular movies are based. *Born on the Fourth of July* closes out the film sequence with a return to the issues and characters of *The Odyssey,* but with a greater sense of the causes and consequences of the war than appears in either *Coming Home* or *First Blood.* The main character completes the task that has eluded the main characters of nearly all of the movies that have come before: he finds a meaningful place in the world apart from the battlefield. There is finally resolution and closure.

Doves and Hawks Rewrite *The Odyssey*

Like *The Odyssey* before it, *Coming Home* is the story of a military officer who goes off to war while his wife is pursued by a number of suitors at home. In Homer's epic poem, Odysseus returns home after ten years of war and ten years of wandering at sea, and finds that Penelope has successfully resisted the suitors. Odysseus is a clever talker and a devious survivor who suffers from bad legs because of the time he has spent at sea. With the help of his son, Telemachus, and with his own mighty bow, he kills all of the suitors in a violent and bloody slaughter and is joyously reunited with his loyal and courageous wife. In *Coming Home*'s version of Homer's classic, things don't work out so neatly. Bob Hyde (Bruce Dern), a Marine Corps officer who wants to be a combat hero, accidentally shoots himself in the leg in Vietnam while going to the latrine. He comes home limping and humiliated, only to discover that his wife, Sally (Jane Fonda), has become sexually involved with an injured Vietnam veteran, Luke Mar-

tin (Jon Voight), a very clever talker and a devious survivor who is a
paraplegic confined to a wheelchair. Luke has turned Sally against the
war and caused her to question almost everything about her life. Hyde
understandably starts to fall apart—this is not, after all, what happened to Odysseus—and when he threatens Sally and Luke with his
rifle, Luke talks him into putting the gun down, explaining that the
time for killing is over. Hyde is shaken, then comforted by Sally, but
as the movie ends he is shown at the beach neatly taking off all of his
clothes and then swimming away by himself. The beginning of *The
Odyssey*, Odysseus lost at sea and in big trouble, is the ending of
Coming Home.

Almost all of the fundamental elements of *The Odyssey* reappear
here, although they are now rearranged to celebrate peace rather than
war: the military officer, the war, his weapon, the clever talker, the
problem with walking, the wife, the suitors, the water, coming home.
But there is now no murder of the suitors, no act of violence at home.
This is a major change from Homer's story. In *The Odyssey* Penelope
is surrounded by noisy and unruly men who fill her house, desire her
loyalty, and try to become her lovers. She does not give in. In *Coming
Home* Sally is surrounded by noisy and unruly men who fill the VA
hospital where she works as a volunteer, and although they all desire
her loyalty, only Luke tries to become her lover. She gives in. This is
clearly a significant revision of *The Odyssey*. Odysseus, with his serious limp, uses his powerful weapon to destroy the suitors, but Hyde,
with his trivial limp, cannot use his. But it is Luke rather than Hyde
who is the clever talker, the devious survivor, and the man with serious
leg troubles, and it may be Luke, rather than Hyde, who is the real
heir to Odysseus here. Strong, charming, and deeply principled, Luke
chains himself to the entrance gates of a military base to protest the
war, speaks out against the war at a high school assembly, and knows
how to get Hyde to put his rifle down. And although he is crippled,
he can sexually satisfy Sally, something Hyde has never been able to
do. But Sally decides to stay with Hyde at the end of the movie, becoming in her own way a badly confused Penelope, since she certainly
appears to love Luke. But there is no resolution for Hyde. Nothing
that Odysseus has done is available to him except the return to the
sea, and that seems to lead nowhere.

Four years later, Sylvester Stallone starred in *First Blood*, an altogether different *Odyssey* and an obvious rebuttal to *Coming Home*.

There is no Penelope figure this time around—in fact, no woman of any consequence—but there is plenty of violence and carnage. *Coming Home* highlights and revises Penelope's role in the story and eliminates Odysseus's slaughter of the suitors; *First Blood* highlights Odysseus's slaughter of his enemies at home and eliminates the role of Penelope. John Rambo does what Bob Hyde cannot do—strike back as Odysseus strikes back—and in that respect at least, *First Blood* is closer to the Homeric original. However, Rambo is just as confused as Hyde at the end of all the carnage, and neither man finds the vindication and victory achieved by Odysseus. Although the Left and Right disagree on which parts of *The Odyssey* are the most meaningful, they agree on the basic predicament of the returning soldier.

Like *The Odyssey*, *First Blood* is the story of a much-decorated military hero who returns home from war to face a very different kind of danger and hostility. Odysseus has been gone from Ithaca so long that everyone, save for his wife and son, assumes he is dead; John Rambo (Sylvester Stallone) returns from Vietnam to discover that everybody wishes he were dead or at least gone from their lives. Disguised as a poor traveler, Odysseus makes his way carefully over the rural countryside of Ithaca as he seeks out old friends and tries to figure out how to deal with the suitors who have taken over his house. He is the lone survivor of the soldiers who left Troy with him. Dressed as a poor traveler and suffering from severe depression and flashbacks to the war, John Rambo comes to the rural countryside of Oregon to visit the only other surviving member of his special forces platoon and to try to figure out what he should do. Odysseus finds friends and allies ready to help; by contrast, Rambo learns that his friend has died from a cancer caused by Agent Orange. Still in disguise, Odysseus enters his own house for the first time and is treated cruelly by the suitors, who don't recognize him. They don't like the way he looks and warn him away. Also dressed poorly, Rambo wanders off toward the nearby town but is warned away by a sheriff, who doesn't like the way he looks. Odysseus refuses to be intimidated and, with the help of Telemachus, goes on a wild rampage of murder and revenge. Rambo refuses to be intimidated even when he is arrested and beaten up in jail, and after he escapes he single-handedly kills large numbers of the police and national guardsmen who are pursuing him. Having killed all of the suitors with his mighty bow and filled his house with their mangled limbs and blood, Odysseus is joyfully reunited with Penelope. Having nearly destroyed the entire town with a series of spectacular explosions and machine-gun attacks and come very close to murdering the sheriff, Rambo collapses in the arms of his former special forces commander. Penelope comforts Odysseus, who tells her about his experiences in Troy. The special forces commander listens uncomfortably as Rambo tells him of a particularly gruesome combat memory, about a best friend who died in his arms just as his legs were blown off, and then leads Rambo off to the waiting police. *First Blood* is just as bleak and dismal an *Odyssey* as *Coming Home*, but for very different reasons.

Hyde and Rambo are both in terrible shape at the end of their respective odysseys—Hyde because the time for killing is over, Rambo because he hasn't gotten the message at all. Hyde is weak, confused, and surrounded by antiwar liberals; Rambo is strong, confused, and surrounded by police and corpses. Luke articulates the stupidity and evil of the war in Vietnam; by contrast, the various military and paramilitary fighters who oppose Rambo share his love of fighting and violence. Dove and hawk have each rewritten *The Odyssey*, but although Hyde's story is over, Rambo will appear again in *Rambo: First Blood, Part II*, when he refights *The Iliad*. Homer is in the process of becoming the apologist for the political Right.

The Deerslayer versus The Heart of Darkness

If *Coming Home* and *First Blood* are radically opposed revisions of the same basic story, *The Deer Hunter* and *Apocalypse Now* are revisions of radically opposed stories, *The Deerslayer* and *The Heart of Darkness*. Cimino adapts Cooper's traditional action-adventure story about heroic white fighters and savage Indians in the woods of New York state for his movie about Vietnam; Coppola re-presents Conrad's modernist irony about savage white men in the Congo and the African natives who are their victims. There is horror enough to go around in both versions, as Cimino and Coppola raise the stakes in the debate over Vietnam. We are now being asked a very important question—not what happened to our soldiers when they came home from Vietnam, but what happened to them in Vietnam. Following Cooper, Cimino tells us that American soldiers were heroic survivors and pathetic victims of sadistic murderous natives, but Coppola, following Conrad, tells us that American soldiers became the sadistic torturers and murderers of the natives and of each other.

Like Cooper's deerslayer, Natty Bumppo, Cimino's deer hunter, Michael Vronsky (Robert DeNiro), is a natural leader of men and an accomplished hunter who is most at home in the forests of the northeastern United States. Bumppo becomes involved in the Indian wars in upstate New York in the 1740s, along with two close friends; Vronsky leaves the forests of western Pennsylvania to fight in Vietnam in the 1960s, along with his two buddies, Steven (John Savage) and Nick (Christopher Walken). Vronsky's friends, like Bumppo's before them, are physically and morally weaker than the central character who looks after them, and eventually they suffer the consequences. Each set of friends is also involved in an uneasy lovers' triangle: Nick loves Linda (Meryl Streep), the beautiful woman who pursues Vronsky, just as one of Bumppo's friends loves Judith Hutter, the beautiful woman who pursues Bumppo. And just as Bumppo rejects this woman for reasons that are never fully explained, Vronsky keeps his emotional distance from Linda. Both heroes are truly comfortable only in the company of other men.

But it is the confrontation between white man and savage that is at the center of both stories. In one of the most powerful moments in Cimino's film, Vronsky and his friends are forced to play Russian roulette by sadistic Vietnamese captors, who torture them in a makeshift river prison and make bets on the outcome. As heads explode around them, Vronsky helps Steven and Nick survive the terror, then takes a weapon that he has tricked his captors into filling with bullets and turns it on them, killing as many as he can. In the midst of this carnage, the friends make their escape. In the comparable scene in *The Deerslayer*, Bumppo is being held prisoner by hostile Indians and when he rejects their request that he marry into their tribe, his primary tormentor angrily hurls a tomahawk at him. Catching it deftly in midair, Bumppo sends it flying back into the man's head and in the confusion that follows he makes his escape. Vronsky leads his friends in a long and difficult escape down the river, but Steven is crippled when American forces bungle the attempt to rescue them by helicopter and Nick is so traumatized that he later deserts the army in order to play Russian roulette in Saigon. Bumppo is recaptured as *The Deerslayer* continues, tied to a tree, and forced to endure a barrage of tomahawks and bullets until he is finally rescued by a squadron of British soldiers. The savage and brutal natives of Vietnam, it seems, are really the savage and brutal natives of North America. But although nothing much has changed about the racist nature of evil, good is having a much harder time of it in Vietnam: the American military fails to accomplish there what the British military accomplished so easily in Bumppo's time, the clean rescue of white prisoners.

The sobering and horrible moments of Russian roulette in *The Deer Hunter* seem to carry a powerful truth about U.S. involvement in Vietnam: that we have been maimed beyond despair by the savages of Southeast Asia. Good (white) American boys are no match for the bad (native) Vietnamese sadists who have been waiting for them there. But *The Deer Hunter* is really only an imaginative recasting of Cooper's imaginative recreation of what never happened anywhere, since *The Deerslayer*, written in 1841, is a novel set in 1740, not a document with any claim to historical veracity. Nevertheless, Cimino's movie became for audiences at the time a political statement about what happened to ordinary American working-class men when they went off to fight in Vietnam. Such was the impressive power of James Fenimore Cooper.

Coppola responded the following year with *Apocalypse Now*, an adaptation of Conrad's *Heart of Darkness*, which neatly refutes Cimino's adaptation of Cooper and makes its debt to Conrad obvious. There is no way we can mistake this for the literal truth. If we have been maimed beyond despair in Vietnam, Coppola asserts, it is because we turned out to be the savages, just as Conrad told us that Europeans had become in Africa almost a century before. Captain Willard (Martin Sheen) works his way upriver in Vietnam on orders of his military superiors to kill the renegade American, Colonel Kurtz (Marlon Brando), who has gone spectacularly bad, just as in Conrad's story the merchant seaman Charlie Marlow works his way upriver in the Congo to find and rescue Mr. Kurtz, the renegade chief of the inner station in charge of gathering ivory, who has also gone spectacularly bad. But the horror that Marlow finds there, the human heads set up on posts and the evidence that the dying Kurtz has taken part in some unspeakable rites, isn't nearly as difficult as the horror waiting for Willard, who finds all this and then is tortured by Kurtz before finally killing him. Willard has these experiences in *Apocalypse Now* not because they happen to Marlow—they do not—but because they happen to Vronsky, who is tortured in *The Deer Hunter* before finally killing his tormentor. Vronsky's antagonist is a mean, sadistic, and monstrous Vietnamese officer, while Willard's is an exemplary American officer, one of the best and brightest, who has become mean, sadistic, and monstrous because he has been given almost unlimited power and respect in Vietnam. We have met the enemy and he is us. Vronsky kills his tormentor and survives intact, and may even be a better man for it, since he returns from Vietnam unable to hunt deer, firing his rifle into the air when one particularly noble-looking buck comes into range. (Bumppo, in the comparable moments in *The Deerslayer*, feels badly about shooting an eagle and refuses to shoot an Indian who is in the process of reloading his rifle.) Willard, on the other hand, starts turning into Kurtz as soon as he kills him, and in a series of striking images we begin to see physical resemblances between the two men. In what can only be a not-so-subtle dig at Cimino, Coppola points his camera at the ritual slaughter of an ox while Willard hacks away at Kurtz offscreen. So much for Vronsky's refusal to shoot a deer.

The Faerie Queene versus The Iliad

It is in this context that George Lucas turns his *Star Wars* movies to the war in Vietnam. His close friend and mentor, Coppola, was unable to explain exactly how or why a good soldier went bad, but Lucas was able to craft a much more credible analysis, rewriting the second episode of his *Star Wars* trilogy, *The Empire Strikes Back*, according to the second book of Spenser's epic poem *The Faerie Queene*. All of Spenser's knights must master Christian spirituality in order to be successful in battle, and in the second book in particular Spenser's knight Guyon must control anger, fear, lust, greed, and selfishness in order to avoid being destroyed by the dark side. Lucas made this into the central plot of *The Empire Strikes Back*, which appeared one year after *Apocalypse Now*. Vader and the evil emperor try to corrupt the good knight, Luke Skywalker, and turn him to the dark side, just as Kurtz has tried to corrupt Willard in Coppola's movie. Unlike Willard, Luke does not succumb to evil and turn into his father, in large measure because he has what Willard does not have, a series of wise teachers. Yoda warns Luke that he can only avoid the dark side by remaining calm and passive, never giving in to fear, anger, or hatred, and fighting only in defense, lessons neither Kurtz nor Willard has learned, schooled as they are by the American military. These are, however, exactly the lessons Sir Guyon learns in a series of adventures in Book Two of *The Faerie Queene*, when he meets the allegorical figures of Occasion and Furor, along with the constantly angry knights Pyrochles and Cymochles. Any knight who gives in to fear, anger, or hatred loses out very badly in Spenser, a lesson taught to Guyon over and over again. At the end of the *Star Wars* movies, Luke successfully turns his father away from the dark side, redeeming the man Obi Wan Kenobi calls "twisted and evil" with unlimited love and the willingness to sacrifice himself. It is Spenser, rather than Conrad, who can explain Vietnam.

The next stage of this debate takes place between Lucas in the *Star Wars* movies and Sylvester Stallone in *Rambo: First Blood, Part II*. Just as *Star Wars* is a meticulously crafted variation on *The Faerie Queene*, so *Rambo: First Blood, Part II* is a meticulously crafted variation on *The Iliad*. What is at issue in this epic argument between Lucas and Stallone is the broadest possible question about the war, not what happens to a soldier when he comes home or who really are the savages or what causes a good soldier to go bad, but who are the winners and which side is worthy of the heroic celebration? The Left wins decisively in *Star Wars*, the Right in *Rambo*, and, not surprisingly, the *Star Wars* trilogy and *Rambo* have been the most popular movies ever made about the war in Vietnam.

Rambo: First Blood, Part II is a story about the rage of a powerful American foot soldier, John Rambo, at the end of a long and horrible war in Vietnam, *The Iliad* a story about the wrath of a powerful Greek military leader, Achilles, at the end of a long and horrible war in Troy. The two warriors have nearly identical adventures. Rambo struggles against a selfish and incompetent commander, Marshall Murdock, just as Achilles struggles against his selfish and incompetent commander, Agamemnon, the Greek general in charge of the war in Troy. Rambo is guided by a friendly father figure, his old special forces commander, Colonel Trautman, just as Achilles is guided by his friendly father figure, the Greek general Phoinix. Rambo experiences the death of a close friend and comrade in arms, a Vietnamese woman named Co, and goes on a murderous rampage following her death, just as Achilles experiences the death of his close friend and comrade in arms, Patroclus, and goes on a murderous rampage following his

death. Rambo rescues the living American POWs, captured by the
Vietnamese and badly mistreated, just as Achilles recovers the body
of the dead Patroclus, captured by the Trojans and badly mistreated.
And at the end Rambo finally comes to terms with the powerful forces
of the American government that control his life, just as Achilles comes
to terms with the powerful forces of the Greek gods that control his.
Although there is a significant difference between the divine forces that
finally help the Greeks in Troy and the selfish traitors who seem to be
in charge of U.S. foreign policy in Vietnam, Achilles is just as powerless before the one as Rambo is before the other.

Because the Greeks finally win the victory at Troy but the Americans lose the war in Vietnam, there is a shift in perspective. *Rambo*
represents *The Iliad* as seen from the loser's point of view, and perhaps
for that reason warriors don't have the same stature as in the Homeric
original. Greek soldiers gain honor by fighting in Troy, but American
soldiers gain dishonor by fighting in Vietnam. Achilles is a powerful
and respected leader of men, at the very top of the hierarchy in Greek
society, but Rambo is at the very bottom of the hierarchy in American
society, not a general but an ex-con scorned by everyone. Although
Rambo is the loser's epic of a bad time for soldiers, its emphasis is not
so much on the war in Vietnam we lost as on the new fight we win
by finding and freeing the POWs left behind, a project that also gives
Rambo the opportunity for killing, maiming, and blowing up as many
of the enemy as he can find. That is what Achilles does when he wins
the war for the Greeks.

But what is perhaps most remarkable about *Rambo* is that it is
simultaneously a careful retelling of *The Iliad* and a systematic refu-
tation of *Star Wars*. In the *Star Wars* trilogy Lucas celebrates the victory of a small band of youthful rebels led by Luke Skywalker and
their primitive third-world allies, who struggle valiantly against an
evil, all-powerful Empire that is trying to control the entire universe
with lethal high-tech weapons. Traditional American values have been
almost totally lost in this totalitarian state, which has corrupted Luke's
father, Darth Vader, and is ruled by a particularly unsavory and uncharismatic emperor modeled on Richard Nixon. Everything finally
depends upon the courage and skills of young Skywalker, the last Jedi
knight in the world and the only hope for a return to freedom and
liberal democratic values. He has to master the spiritual Force of the
universe, the ability to use his mind. Fortunately, all of the lethal high-

tech weapons the Empire relies on are grossly overrated and never work as they are supposed to. In a striking right-wing revision of this story, Stallone celebrates the victory of a lone, much maligned American foot soldier, John Rambo, and his single third-world ally, the Vietnamese woman, who struggle valiantly against an evil, all-powerful conspiracy of savage Vietnamese, sadistic Russians, and corrupt self-serving Americans, who put their trust in lethal high-tech weapons. Traditional American values have been almost totally lost in Rambo's United States, a nightmarish bureaucratic state that has corrupted Rambo's old commander, Colonel Trautman, and is ruled by a particularly unsavory and uncharismatic Washington official, Marshall Murdock, who represents the will of the liberal Democrats who control the U.S. Congress. Everything finally depends upon the courage and skill of John Rambo, the last real soldier in America and the only hope for a return to freedom and conservative Republican values. He is a powerful fighting force who believes that his mind is his best weapon. Fortunately, all of the lethal high-tech weapons of the liberal state are grossly overrated and never work as they are supposed to.

Which story is the greater fantasy? It may be comforting to know that the Right's nightmare about the Left is virtually identical to the Left's nightmare about the Right, but there are subtle differences between the endings of these two mirror-image stories that reveal that the Right is more fearful and paranoid about the future than the Left. The emperor is dead and his Empire in ruins at the end of Lucas's story, but the bureaucrat and his bureaucracy are still triumphant at the end of Stallone's. The evil emperor betrays Luke's friends in *Star Wars*, luring them into a trap he is sure will destroy them all, while he shoots electricity into Luke, causing him to writhe about on the floor. What this not-too-smart emperor doesn't count on is that Darth Vader will turn against him for this betrayal and torture of Luke, and will kill him. In Stallone's version of all this, the evil bureaucrat Marshall Murdock betrays Rambo, abandoning him to the enemy when Rambo finds evidence that American liberals will not allow anyone to know that our POWs are alive and waiting to be rescued. Murdock is sure that Rambo will be destroyed. The enemy tortures Rambo by the usual creative methods, one of which involves shooting electricity into him through some old bedsprings, which causes him to writhe about. What the not-too-smart Murdock does not count on is that Trautman will turn against him for this betrayal and torture of

Rambo, but Trautman, who is no Darth Vader, rebels very meekly and gives Rambo very little help. Rambo fights savagely with Murdock, but although he is willing to give him a big scare with a big knife, he knows better than to kill him. This is a representative of the liberal American bureaucracy, after all. So whereas Luke and his friends happily blow up the Empire's new death star, Rambo angrily machine-guns all of Murdock's fancy computers. Luke and his friends joyfully celebrate their victory but Rambo sulks off by himself, unloved and unappreciated, because liberals have caused good Americans to hate their soldiers.

Unlike many of the other movies about Vietnam, *Rambo* puts forth a revisionist history of the war that seemed to most critics to be little more than a right-wing fantasy. But it was an answer to Lucas's left-wing fantasy, and it was designed, from the beginning, as an answer to Lucas's story of the victory of the American Left and its Vietnamese allies.

Henry IV, Part I

Oliver Stone's *Platoon* stands on its own as a pivotal turning point in this sequence of movies about Vietnam. Stone's first Vietnam movie is an obvious rebuttal to *Rambo*, revealing the weaknesses of Stallone's version of the war, but it is also a critical rejection of the *Star Wars* trilogy and Lucas's version as well. We are in an uneasy political middle ground in the debate between Right and Left over the meaning of the war. Which side is telling us the truth about the war and the warriors? Stone's answer is: neither.

Like *Henry IV, Part I*, which it follows very closely, *Platoon* is the story of a young soldier who is torn between a fanatical superwarrior who lives for bloodshed and a pleasure-loving fighter with no illusions about the nature of war. In Shakespeare's play the fanatical superwarrior is Hotspur, a man who rebels against the king, whom he dismisses as a selfish fool, and fights savagely in a losing battle against him. The pleasure-loving fighter is Falstaff, a man who drinks heavily, hangs out in a tavern filled with his inebriated cronies, and fights reluctantly for the king even though he does not believe in his cause. The man caught between them is Prince Hal, who begins as a laid-back and playful follower of Falstaff but ends as a savage and deadly fighter like Hotspur. In Stone's movie the Hotspur character is Sergeant Barnes (Tom Berenger), a man who fights savagely in the losing battle of the American forces in Vietnam and kills often and without remorse. The Falstaff character is Sergeant Elias (Willem Dafoe), a man who smokes large quantities of dope, hangs out in a barracks room filled with fellow dopers, and fights reluctantly for a cause in which he does not believe. The Prince Hal character is new recruit Chris Taylor (Charlie Sheen), a man who is pulled between them much as Hal is pulled between Hotspur and Falstaff. Stone very neatly transfers the fundamental characters and plot lines of Shakespeare's play to Vietnam, along with some of his smaller touches. Prince Hal is alienated from his father, the king, a veteran of earlier battles, just as Chris Taylor is alienated from his father, a World War II veteran. Falstaff carries a bottle of sherry into battle in place of his pistol, just as Elias uses his rifle as a pipe to smoke dope.

But Stone makes at least one significant change in the plot, which makes *Platoon* a more brutal version of *Henry IV, Part I* and much less hopeful about the fate of the liberal side in Vietnam: Falstaff survives the brutality of war in Shakespeare's play, but the Falstaffian character in *Platoon* does not. When war breaks out between his father and a group of rebels led by Hotspur, Prince Hal turns his back on his tavern life and joins the army. Falstaff comes along with him. In one of the most famous scenes of the play, Falstaff pretends to be dead when he is attacked by one of Hotspur's officers and fools his attacker into leaving the scene. A moment later Prince Hal kills Hotspur, sees Falstaff on the ground, and leaves the battle, convinced that his old friend is dead. Then in an impressive comic resurrection, Falstaff rises, stabs Hotspur's corpse, and begins to carry it off, only to meet up with Hal, who is stunned to see him back from the dead and surprised that he is claiming credit for killing Hotspur. The old trickster is still going strong.

What happens in *Platoon* is somewhat different, although it follows this order of events very closely. Fearful of the testimony the Falstaffian Elias plans to give against him because he has murdered an unarmed Vietnamese civilian, the Hotspur-like Barnes stalks Elias in the jungle and fires his rifle at him at fairly close range. Elias falls to the ground, but given the dangerous situation, Barnes does not stay around to examine his fallen body. When Barnes reports Elias's death to the other soldiers, claiming that the enemy is responsible, Taylor assumes that Barnes must have killed him and does not go back to investigate. But a short time later as the platoon is being airlifted away, Taylor and Barnes see Elias running toward their helicopter, arms upraised in a call for help, as large numbers of North Vietnamese soldiers pursue him. This time the resurrection is tragic but much more powerful, as Elias dies a miserable and painful death in front of them. Much later Taylor kills Barnes in retribution at the end of a terrible battle scene.

What does Stone's variation on Shakespeare do to the meaning of the story? Besides making it grimmer, Stone's change makes much stronger and clearer connections between the events. Hal's killing of Hotspur is only indirectly connected to Falstaff's near death at the hands of Hotspur's ally, but now Taylor kills Barnes because Barnes has tried to kill Elias and is finally responsible for Elias's death. And yet Stone also manages to implicate Taylor. When Falstaff finally dies of a fever in *Henry V*, two sequels later, he has been renounced by Hal and sent to prison. Hal is clearly responsible for his death. When Elias dies in *Platoon*, Barnes and the North Vietnamese soldiers may be primarily responsible, but Taylor understands that by failing to look for Elias, he too shares responsibility for his death. Nothing is clean or simple in Vietnam. Hal goes on to become king, glorying in victory; Taylor goes home to an uncertain future. This is a much grimmer *Henry IV, Part I*.

In Stone's hands, Shakespeare's story becomes a parable of right-wing and left-wing versions of the war in Vietnam. The platoon Taylor joins is divided into two equal factions, one led by the Rambo-type superwarrior Barnes, the other by the Han Solo–type rebel Elias. Barnes is an angry and violent soldier like Rambo, who tortures and kills Vietnamese civilians without any regard for the rules. Like Rambo, he loves fighting, hates the enemy, and kills at every opportunity in impressive displays of strength and power. Elias is another free-thinking rebel like Han Solo, who is totally unsuited to life in the army. Like Han Solo, he is a pleasure-loving egotist and scoundrel who can also be very loyal to his friends. Barnes and Elias compete with each other for Taylor's allegiance, but in this allegory of the fight between the Right and Left over the meaning of Vietnam, neither side finally succeeds, although what happens is dramatic enough. Barnes kills Elias, just as Rambo would almost certainly have killed Han Solo had they ever been in the same platoon together, and Taylor kills Barnes, as the soldier caught in the middle forced to dispense justice. Liberal rebels like Han Solo are the real enemies of right-wing superwarriors like Rambo, Stone tells us, but Lucas and Stallone have both lied to us about the outcome of the battle. Han Solo helps the liberals to glorious victory in *Star Wars*, but in Stone's more realistic movie, Elias is no match for a nearly insane right-wing fighter like Barnes. Rambo single-handedly wins every battle in Vietnam against improbable odds, even when his own commander has turned against him, but in Stone's more realistic movie, Barnes pays the price for turning against his own troops. He is not invincible after all, or even very bulletproof.

Although Stone has encouraged audiences to believe that he based the movie on his own experiences as a young soldier in Vietnam (as if he were Prince Hal!), *Platoon* much more closely describes his experiences as a young filmmaker in Hollywood, joining a platoon of more experienced veteran filmmakers divided into two factions over the meaning of Vietnam, one led by Stallone, the other by Lucas. Stallone and Lucas compete with each other for Stone's allegiance as a filmmaker, just as Barnes and Elias do for Taylor's allegiance as a soldier. Just as Taylor kills Barnes after Barnes has killed Elias, Stone disposes of Stallone after Stallone has disposed of Lucas. *Platoon* is a movie about itself as much as it is about the war, and Taylor's speech at the very end has two meanings, one for Taylor, the other for Stone. "The war is over for me now, but it will always be there—the rest of my days. As I am sure Elias will be—fighting with Barnes for . . . possession of my soul. There are times since I have felt like a child born of these two fathers . . . but be that as it may, those of us who did make it have an obligation to build again, to teach to others what we know and to try with what's left of our lives to find a goodness and meaning to this life." Stone has to move past Stallone and Lucas, just as Taylor has to move past Barnes and Elias, in order to find goodness and meaning in life.

There is one other significant difference between *Henry IV, Part I* and *Platoon*. Shakespeare's play alternates between deeply serious scenes of deceit, betrayal, and murder among the soldiers and broadly comic scenes of deceit, betrayal, and practical joking among the drinkers. Stone's movie is deeply serious all the time, but the next movies in this sequence, Stanley Kubrick's *Full Metal Jacket* and Barry Levinson's *Good Morning, Vietnam*, are not.

All Quiet on the Western Front versus *The Acharnians*

Alternately comic and serious, *Full Metal Jacket* and *Good Morning, Vietnam* are very similar movies about the power of comic attitudes to oppose war, the only fundamental theme of *Henry IV, Part I* ignored by Stone in *Platoon*. Although both movies present liberal positions on the war, they disagree completely on the results. The question is no longer which soldiers won the war, the issue of *Star Wars* and *Rambo*, but how soldiers opposed it. Based on *All Quiet on the Western Front*, Erich Maria Remarque's antiwar novel of World War I, Stanley Kubrick's movie *Full Metal Jacket* is the story of Private Joker (Matthew Modine), a peace-button-wearing soldier and self-styled comedian who chafes at the false information he must report as news for the armed forces newspaper, *Stars and Stripes*, stands up to his superior officers, and gets in trouble because of it. Based on *The Acharnians*, Aristophanes' antiwar play about the conflicts between Athens and Sparta in the fifth century B.C., Barry Levinson's movie *Good Morning, Vietnam* is the story of Adrian Cronauer (Robin Williams), a peace-loving soldier and self-styled comedian who chafes at the false information he must report as news for armed forces radio, stands up to his superior officers, and gets in trouble because of it. Both men joke about the army and the war, and although this entertains their fellow soldiers, it irritates their superior officers, who send them, as punishment, into dangerous areas of Vietnam where they are nearly killed, Joker in combat, Cronauer in a minefield. Both survive but are changed by the experience. Joker kills the enemy soldier who has killed a number of American soldiers at the end of *Full Metal Jacket*; Cronauer saves the life of the enemy soldier who has killed American soldiers at the end of *Good Morning, Vietnam*. The difference is crucial: Joker drops his opposition to the war at this moment, becoming like all the other soldiers around him, whereas Cronauer becomes increasingly opposed to the war and is quickly discharged from the army so he cannot influence the other soldiers around him. Both movies are concerned with the brutalities, stupidities, and lies of war, and the place of a truth-speaking comedian who cannot take any of it very seriously, but if Joker and Cronauer are heirs of Falstaff, they end up illustrating different truths. The war corrupts Joker and turns him into a soldier; the only favor he can do for the enemy is to kill her. The war cannot corrupt Cronauer, although in the eyes of the army he is guilty of treason; the only favor he can do for himself and the enemy is to make his own private peace. *Good Morning, Vietnam* is the upbeat, positive version of *Full Metal Jacket*.

Although *Full Metal Jacket* takes some of its material from Gustav Hansford's novel *The Short Timers*, the acknowledged source of the movie, Kubrick is much more significantly indebted to Erich Maria Remarque's classic antiwar novel about World War I, *All Quiet on the Western Front*, especially Louis Milestone's 1930 film version of the novel. Both movies begin with very long sections that show new recruits being turned into soldiers by extremely sadistic drill sergeants, and both continue with extended scenes of soldiers enduring enemy attacks in combat, focusing on the moment when the main character kills an enemy soldier at close hand for the first time. It is a horrible trauma for both of them. Kubrick moves Milestone's movie to Vietnam and increases the level of suffering and brutality it portrays, but he also includes a more upbeat ending. Remarque's German recruits endure constant abuse from their sadistic drillmaster and finally take their revenge, catching him late at night, wrapping him up in a blanket, and beating him badly. The drillmaster treats them more carefully afterward. Kubrick's American recruits endure constant abuse from their sadistic drill sergeant and take out their anger and frustration on a goofy fellow recruit, catching him late at night, wrapping him up in a blanket, and beating him badly. The drill sergeant does not treat them more carefully afterward, and the goofy misfit eventually snaps from the level of abuse, killing the drill sergeant and committing suicide while Private Joker watches. What's bad enough in Milestone's film is many times more terrible in Kubrick's.

In the second half of Milestone's film the novel's main character kills a French soldier who has run into a ditch in which he has taken refuge during a fierce battle. The French soldier dies slowly, traumatizing the repentant young hero of the movie, who shares his ditch with the body for a long time. He even decides that although they are enemies he did not mean to kill the man, and he promises to do what he can for the corpse's family. In the second half of Kubrick's movie Private Joker kills an enemy soldier with the greatest of difficulty. But Remarque's main character dies in *All Quiet on the Western Front*, along with all of his fellow soldiers, whereas Private Joker is still alive, singing the Mickey Mouse Club song. Remarque's main character dies hating the war and feeling powerless to do anything about it. Joker is learning how to be a soldier.

Levinson responded with his own story about the comedian soldier who refuses to capitulate to the military. Like *The Acharnians, Good Morning, Vietnam* is a comedy about one man's attempt to make peace with his country's enemy and about the importance of comedy in speaking the truth against forces that would oppress it. There are extensive discussions of the function of comedy in both stories. Dikaiopolis speaks the truth in *The Acharnians*, standing up for the principles of comedy, and Cronauer does the same in *Good Morning, Vietnam*. Aristophanes justifies his use of political humor in an earlier comedy that offended the political leadership of Athens, and Cronauer's comic routines cause debates over the nature and purpose of humor at the armed forces radio station where he works. For Aristophanes, as for Levinson, comedy is an effective way of opposing the war. Dikaiopolis makes peace with the Spartans in *The Acharnians*, and although he is accused of treason in the process, when he humiliates the army's greatest soldier the other Athenians come around to his side. They see how much money he is making by trading with the enemy and how many dancing girls are happy to entertain him. Adrian Cronauer almost accomplishes these same feats in *Good Morning, Vietnam*, making friends with Vietnamese civilians whom the rest of the army despises and thoroughly humiliating his superior officers, but when his Vietnamese friend is revealed to be a Viet Cong terrorist who has killed American soldiers, Cronauer is accused of treason, discharged from the armed forces, and ordered home. Dikaiopolis is celebrated as a hero at the end of *The Acharnians*, but Cronauer has much more limited success at the end of *Good Morning, Vietnam*. His peace is not quite so wide-ranging, wonderful, or appreciated, although he has done exactly what Dikaiopolis has done. His Vietnamese friend protects Cronauer from being killed by the Viet Cong, and Cronauer protects his Vietnamese friend from being killed by the U.S. Army. They have made their own private peace.

The Odyssey One More Time

What Cronauer failed to accomplish in *Good Morning, Vietnam* in 1988, Ron Kovic achieved in *Born on the Fourth of July* in 1989: successful public opposition to the war. The story of Vietnam veteran

Ron Kovic, *Born on the Fourth of July* returns us to the issues of *The Odyssey* from the very beginning of this debate about Vietnam. Although it was not produced until 1989, the film was originally written by Oliver Stone in 1978, the same year as *Coming Home*, and is extremely similar to Hal Ashby's film. Once again a handsome soldier is severely injured in Vietnam and returns home a paraplegic, gradually turning against the war while he is indifferently treated in a VA hospital. Saved by brief contact with a woman who teaches him how to love her even though he is paralyzed from the waist down, the soldier regains some of his old strength and self-respect, and by the end of the movie he is able to speak out angrily and effectively against the war. The story of Luke Martin in *Coming Home* is the story of Ron Kovic (Tom Cruise) in *Born on the Fourth of July*, although we are now told much more about the wheelchair-bound veteran, about how his childhood and family life affected his willingness to fight for his country, and how his combat experiences in Vietnam and his treatment in a VA hospital affected his willingness to fight for peace. We are back to *The Odyssey* and to the issues debated by the antiwar *Coming Home* in 1978 and the prowar *First Blood* in 1982, but we now have a much more complete treatment of Homer's story. Whereas *Coming Home* revises Penelope's role and eliminates Odysseus's killing of the suitors, and *First Blood* revises Odysseus's killing of the suitors but eliminates the role of Penelope, both parts of *The Odyssey* are present finally in *Born on the Fourth of July*. Ron Kovic tries desperately to regain his childhood sweetheart only to discover that she has no interest in cripples. Then he fights back against the men and women who would stop him from speaking out against the war, taking his opposition to the war to the Republication National Convention in 1972, then returning as an invited speaker at the Democratic National Convention in 1976. Inspired by his reading of *Johnny Got His Gun*, the real Ron Kovic tells us in his preface to Dalton Trumbo's antiwar classic that he vowed to accomplish what eluded Trumbo's deaf, dumb, and blind quadraplegic: to turn himself into a symbol of war. As he succeeds Kovic finds purpose and meaning in his life beyond that of being a soldier.

The image with which *Born on the Fourth of July* ends, Kovic about to address the Democratic convention as a hero, marks his full acceptance back into American society—the real coming home that eludes Luke Martin, John Rambo, Michael Vronsky, Captain Willard,

Private Joker, Adrian Cronauer—everyone, in fact, except for the lucky heroes of *Star Wars*, who got to fight on the winning side from the beginning. There may be no final word about Vietnam, but by returning us to the issues of *Coming Home, First Blood*, and *Platoon* and explaining the issues more clearly and forcefully, *Born on the Fourth of July* ends a decade of intense debate about the meaning of the war, a debate that depends on Homer, Aristophanes, Spenser, Shakespeare, Cooper, and Conrad as much as on what really happened in Vietnam.

CHAPTER 13

Matthew Arnold Meets Godzilla

Popular entertainment has always been an easy target for critics, who claim that it demeans us, confuses our impressionable children, cheapens everything it comes in contact with, and represents a terrible loss of core human values. "What has happened to Matthew Arnold's 'best which has been thought and said,' F. R. Leavis's 'great tradition,' T. S. Eliot's 'ideal order,' and all the other dreams of an enduring Eurocentric culture beloved by the intelligentsia?" James Twitchell asks plaintively in *Carnival Culture: The Trashing of Taste in America*, one of the most thorough of the recent attacks on popular entertainment (8). Twitchell's answer is finally that writers, producers, and corporate executives have learned that they can make the most money by appealing to the very worst in all of us. Instead of uplifting, inspiring, and improving—what the great nineteenth-century critic Matthew Arnold ("Culture and Anarchy") claimed as the function of all great art and literature—contemporary entertainment only demeans, denigrates, and destroys.

If Twitchell is right, we are in deep trouble; we might appropriately title his story "Matthew Arnold Meets Godzilla," with the part of the overgrown gorilla being played by the entertainment industry. But although it is true that in the animated short film *Bambi Meets Godzilla* the gentle and cuddly fawn is crushed by the foot of the cartoon monster just as the story is about to begin, in "Matthew Arnold Meets Godzilla" the relationship between the varieties of storytelling these individuals represent is much more involved and much more interesting. Godzilla does not trample Matthew Arnold to death in the back alleys of civilization, as some have feared, although he does rewrite the great literature of the past according to his own set of values. Literature is transformed but not destroyed by popular culture. Matthew Arnold and Godzilla are fellow travelers in the long and diverse history of storytelling.

In *Fahrenheit 451* Ray Bradbury warns us about the coming destruction of the great books, that sometime in the not too distant future no one will be allowed to read Shakespeare or Swift or Matthew Arnold or the Bible, and firemen will be employed in burning what few books remain as well as any people who may get in their way. Instead of reading, people will take great pleasure in watching and interacting with their parlor families, life-size television characters who will act out emotionally engrossing but otherwise worthless stories that will be projected into their lives by room-size television environments. Instead of thinking, people will listen to the constant and inescapable drone of advertising and to music that will be piped into their ears by tiny seashell-shaped devices, and they will slowly be destroyed. Some will try to commit suicide, never understanding what is happening to them; some will drive their cars much too fast in order to feel alive, and kill many people along the way; and some will go to war and destroy entire civilizations. It is a sobering cautionary tale, and one much loved by readers of literature because in Bradbury's world, without Shakespeare, Swift, Arnold, and the Bible we all die. The novel is not without hope, however, for a few heroic souls stand up to the destruction of our cultural heritage, memorizing bits and pieces of the classics so they can be preserved for a better time.

Bradbury published *Fahrenheit 451* in 1953 at the very beginning of the age of television, and by now his story seems very prescient. "This book describes a world peopled with young folk who have bypassed reading and writing and who thus have been forced to fabricate a life without benefit of that innermost, intimate guide, the self," Barry Sanders warned us recently in *A is for Ox: Violence, Electronic Media, and the Silencing of the Written Word.* "It does not take a powerful imagination to describe such a world. The details can be found in the morning newspaper. It is a world marked by pain and death, a world filled with despair and drop-outs, teen-age suicides, gang killings, broken homes, and homicides" (xi–xii). "If a person turns from print—

finding it too slow, too hard, irrelevant to the excitements of the present," Sven Birkerts asks in *The Gutenberg Elegies*, "then what happens to that person's sense of culture and continuity?" (20). The answer, for Birkerts, is that these are completely lost, along with a sense of what it means to be a human being. "Only a few handfuls of students now enter Yale with an authentic passion for reading," Harold Bloom complains in *The Western Canon*. "You cannot teach someone to love poetry if they come to you without such love. How can you teach solitude?" (485). The result for Bloom will be the destruction of university English departments.

Books are dangerous, Bradbury told us in 1953, because they tell the truth, which means that they are full of the kind of material that makes people unhappy. But in the middle of his story Bradbury says something I find much more interesting. "It's not books you need," an old, wise, book-reading man tells the hero of the story, "it's some of the things that once were in books." Because his speech anticipates the position I have taken in this book, I take some consolation in it and offer it here:

The same things *could* be in the "parlor families" today. The same infinite detail and awareness could be projected through the radios and televisions, but are not. No, no, it's not books at all you're looking for! Take it where you can find it, in old phonograph records, old motion pictures, and in old friends; look for it in nature and look for it in yourself. Books were only one type of receptacle where we stored a lot of things we were afraid we might forget. There is nothing magical in them at all. The magic is only in what books say, how they stitched the patches of the universe together into one garment for us. (82–83)

It is a proposition worth examining with some care, given the dire predictions that surround us about the coming dark age. "If literature and the other arts are to play some meaningful part in social life in years to come," Alvin Kernan writes in *The Death of Literature*, "their relationship to the established order needs to be thought through again and redefined" (31). But literature is crucially important for society today, just as it always has been; the problem is that critics like Kernan can no longer recognize literature, and that is our great loss because we need their insight. Our libraries are full of brilliant critical interpretations of great works of literature that virtually no one reads. Our lives are full of compelling and powerful stories that virtually no one writes about. It is time to bring the two together.

Works Cited

Arendt, Hannah. "Society and Culture." In *Culture for the Millions? Mass Media in Modern Society*, ed. Norman Jacobs, pp. 43–52. Princeton: D. Van Nostrand, 1959.

Aristophanes. *Lysistrata, The Acharnians, The Clouds*. Trans. Alan H. Sommerstein. London: Penguin, 1973.

Aristotle. *The Poetics*. New York: W. W. Norton, 1982.

Arnold, Matthew. "Culture and Anarchy." In *Poetry and Criticism of Matthew Arnold*, ed. A. Dwight Culler, pp. 406–98. Boston: Houghton Mifflin, 1961.

Austen, Jane. *Sense and Sensibility*. London: Penguin, 1972.

Barthes, Roland. "The Photographic Message." In *Image Music Text*, trans. Stephen Heath, pp. 15–31. New York: Hill and Wang, 1977.

Barzun, Jacques. *The Use and Abuse of Art*. Princeton: Princeton University Press, 1973.

Benjamin, Walter. "On Some Motifs in Baudelaire." In *Illuminations*, ed. Hannah Arendt, trans. Harry Zohn, pp. 155–200. New York: Schocken, 1969.

———. "The Work of Art in the Age of Mechanical Reproduction." In *Illuminations*, ed. Hannah Arendt, trans. Harry Zohn, pp. 217–52. New York: Schocken, 1969.

Berger, John. *Ways of Seeing*. London: British Broadcasting Corporation and Penguin Books, 1972.

Birkerts, Sven. *The Gutenberg Elegies: The Fate of Reading in an Electronic Age*. New York: Fawcett Columbine, 1994.

Bloom, Harold. *The Western Canon: The Books and School of the Ages*. New York: Riverhead Books, 1994.

Bourdieu, Pierre. *Distinction: A Social Critique of the Judgment of Taste.* Trans. Richard Nice. Cambridge: Harvard University Press, 1984.

Bradbury, Ray. *Fahrenheit 451.* New York: Ballantine, 1991.

Brereton, Geoffrey. *Principles of Tragedy: A Rational Examination of the Tragic Concept in Life and Literature.* Coral Gables: University of Miami Press, 1969.

Brooks, Peter. *The Melodramatic Imagination: Balzac, Henry James, Melodrama, and the Mode of Excess.* New Haven: Yale University Press, 1976.

Calinescu, Matei. *Faces of Modernity: Avant-Garde, Decadence, Kitsch.* Bloomington: Indiana University Press, 1977.

Campbell, Joseph. *The Hero with a Thousand Faces.* Princeton: Princeton University Press, 1949.

Camus, Albert. "On the Future of Tragedy." In *Lyrical and Critical Essays,* trans. Ellen Conroy Kennedy, pp. 295–310. New York: Random House, 1970.

Castiglione, Baldesar. *The Book of the Courtier.* Trans. Charles S. Singleton. Garden City: Doubleday Anchor, 1959.

Cawelti, John. *The Six-Gun Mystique.* Bowling Green: Bowling Green University Popular Press, 1975.

Charney, Maurice. *Sexual Fiction.* London: Methuen, 1981.

Clark, Kenneth. *The Nude: A Study in Ideal Form.* 1956; reprint Middlesex: Penguin, 1960.

Conrad, Joseph. *The Heart of Darkness.* Ed. Robert Kimbrough. Rev. ed. New York: W. W. Norton, 1972.

Cooper, James Fenimore. *The Deerslayer.* Laurel: Lightyear Press, 1984.

Cowley, Malcolm. *The Literary Situation.* New York: Viking Press, 1954.

Cox, Harvey. "Sex and Secularization." In *The Secular City: Secularization and Urbanization in Theological Perspective,* pp. 167–89. Rev. ed. New York: Macmillan, 1967.

Danto, Arthur. *The Transfiguration of the Commonplace.* Cambridge: Harvard University Press, 1981.

DeLoris, Guillaume, *The Romance of the Rose.* Trans. Harry Tobbins, ed. Charles W. Dunn. New York: Dutton, 1962.

Eco, Umberto. *The Open Work.* Trans. Anna Cancogni. Cambridge: Harvard University Press, 1989.

Eliot, T. S. "Tradition and the Individual Talent." In *The Sacred Wood: Essays on Poetry and Criticism,* pp. 47–59. London: Methuen, 1920.

Enzenberger, Hans Magnus. *The Consciousness Industry: On Literature, Politics and the Media.* New York: Seabury Press, 1974.

Etheredge, George. *The Man of Mode.* Ed. John Barnard. New York: W. W. Norton, 1988.

Euripides. *Hippolytus.* In *Euripides I,* vol. 5 of *The Complete Greek Trage-*

dies, ed. David Greene and Richmond Lattimore, pp. 179–242. Chicago: University of Chicago Press, 1956.

Faas, Ekbert. *Tragedy and After: Euripides, Shakespeare, Goethe*. Kingston: McGill-Queen's University Press, 1984.

Fiske, John. *Television Culture*. 1987; rpt. New York: Routledge, 1989.

Fiske, John, and John Hartley. *Reading Television*. London: Methuen, 1978.

Flaubert, Gustave. *Madame Bovary*. Ed. and trans. Paul DeMan. New York: W. W. Norton, 1965.

Foucault, Michel. *An Introduction*. Vol. 1 of *The History of Sexuality*. Trans. Robert Hurley. New York: Vintage, 1980.

———. *The Uses of Pleasure*. Vol. 2 of *The History of Sexuality*. Trans. Robert Hurley. New York: Vintage, 1986.

Graff, Gerald. *Literature against Itself: Literary Ideas in Modern Society*. Chicago: University of Chicago Press, 1979.

Hall, Stuart. "Notes on Deconstructing 'the Popular.' " In *People's History and Socialist Theory*, ed. R. Samuel, pp. 227–40. London: Routledge & Kegan Paul, 1981.

Hegel, G. W. F. *Hegel on Tragedy*. Ed. Anne and Henry Paolucci. New York: Harper and Row, 1962.

Heilman, Robert Bechtold. *Tragedy and Melodrama: Versions of Experience*. Seattle: University of Washington Press, 1968.

Hirsch, E. D. *Validity in Interpretation*. New Haven: Yale University Press, 1967.

Homer. *The Iliad*. Trans. Richard Lattimore. Chicago: University of Chicago Press, 1951.

———. *The Odyssey*. Trans. Robert Fitzgerald. New York: Random House, 1961.

Huyssen, Andreas. *After the Great Divide: Modernism, Mass Culture, Postmodernism*. Bloomington: Indiana University Press, 1986.

Ibsen, Henrik. *Ghosts*. In *The Complete Major Prose Plays*, trans. Rolf Fjelde, pp. 197–276. New York: Farrar, Straus and Giroux, 1978.

Iser, Wolfgang. *The Implied Reader: Patterns of Communication in Prose Fiction from Bunyan to Beckett*. Baltimore: Johns Hopkins University Press, 1974.

Jameson, Fredric. "Ideology and Utopia in Mass Culture." *Social Text* 1 (1979): 130–48.

———. *The Political Unconscious: Narrative as a Socially Symbolic Act*. Ithaca: Cornell University Press, 1981.

Jaspers, Karl. "Basic Characteristics of the Tragic." In *Tragedy: Vision and Form*, ed. Robert Corrigan, pp. 43–52. San Francisco: Chandler, 1965.

Kernan, Alvin. *The Death of Literature*. New Haven: Yale University Press, 1990.

Krieger, Murray. *The Tragic Vision: Variations on a Theme in Literary In-terpretation*. New York: Holt, Rinehart and Winston, 1960.

Langer, Suzanne. "The Great Dramatic Forms: The Tragic Rhythm." In *Feeling and Form*, pp. 351–66. New York: Scribners, 1953.

Lindberg, Gary. *Edith Wharton and the Novel of Manners*. Charlottesville: University Press of Virginia, 1975.

Lukacs, George. *History and Class Consciousness: Studies in Marxist Dialectics*. Trans. Rodney Livingstone. Cambridge: MIT Press, 1971.

Macdonald, Dwight. "Masscult and Midcult." In *Against the American Grain: Essays on the Effects of Mass Culture*, pp. 3–75. New York: Random House, 1962.

Mannheim, Karl. *Ideology and Utopia: An Introduction to the Sociology of Knowledge*. Trans. Louis Wirth and Edward Shils. New York: Harcourt, Brace, and World, n.d.

Marcuse, Herbert. *Eros and Civilization: A Philosophical Inquiry into Freud*. Boston: Beacon Press, 1956.

———. "On Hedonism." In *Negations: Essays in Critical Theory*, trans. Jeremy J. Shapiro, pp. 159–200. Boston: Beacon Press, 1968.

———. *One Dimensional Man: Studies in the Ideology of Advanced Industrial Society*. Boston: Beacon Press, 1964.

McCollom, William G. *Tragedy*. New York: Macmillan, 1957.

McLuhan, Marshall. "Television in a New Light." In *The Meaning of Commercial Television: The Texas Stanford Seminar*, ed. Stanley T. Donner, pp. 87–107. Austin: University of Texas Press, 1967.

———. *Understanding Media: The Extensions of Man*. New York: Mentor, 1964.

Mitchell, W. J. T. *Iconology: Image, Text, Ideology*. Chicago: University of Chicago Press, 1986.

More, Thomas. *Utopia*. Trans. Robert M. Adams. New York: W. W. Norton, 1975.

Mumford, Lewis. *Art and Technics*. New York: Columbia University Press, 1952.

Nietzsche, Friedrich. "The Birth of Tragedy." In *Basic Writings of Nietzsche*, ed. Walter Kaufmann, pp. 3–144. New York: Modern Library, 1966.

Pirandello, Luigi. *Six Characters in Search of an Author*. In *Naked Masks: Five Plays by Luigi Pirandello*, ed. Eric Bentley, trans. Edward Storer, pp. 211–76. New York: E. P. Dutton, 1952.

Pollock, Dale. *Skywalking: The Life and Films of George Lucas*. New York: Harmony Books, 1983.

Postman, Neil. *Amusing Ourselves to Death: Public Discourse in the Age of Show Business*. New York: Penguin, 1985.

Rebhorn, Wayne. *Courtly Performances: Masking and Festivity in Casti-*

glione's "Book of the Courtier." Detroit: Wayne State University Press, 1978.

Remarque, Erich Maria. *All Quiet on the Western Front.* Trans. A. W. Wheen. New York: Ballantine, 1982.

Ross, Andrew. *No Respect: Intellectuals and Popular Culture.* New York: Routledge, 1989.

Sanders, Barry. *A is for Ox: Violence, Electronic Media, and the Silencing of the Written Word.* New York: Pantheon, 1994.

Scheler, Max. "On the Tragic." In *Tragedy: Vision and Form,* ed. Robert Corrigan, pp. 3–18. San Francisco: Chandler, 1965.

Scholes, Robert. *Textual Power: Literary Theory and the Teaching of English.* New Haven: Yale University Press, 1985.

Sewall, Richard B. *The Vision of Tragedy.* Enlarged ed. New Haven: Yale University Press, 1980.

Shakespeare, William. *Henry IV, Part I.* Ed. James L. Sanderson. New York: W. W. Norton, 1969.

———. *Much Ado about Nothing.* Ed. Sheldon Zitner. New York: Oxford University Press, 1993.

Spenser, Edmund. *The Faerie Queene.* In *Edmund Spenser's Poetry,* ed. Hugh MacLean and Anne Lake Prescott, pp. 1–460. 3d ed. New York: W. W. Norton, 1993.

Strindberg, August. *Miss Julie.* In *Six Plays of Strindberg,* trans. Elizabeth Sprigge, pp. 59–114. Garden City, N.Y.: Doubleday, 1955.

Strong, Roy. *The Renaissance Garden in England.* London: Thames and Hudson, 1979.

Swift, Jonathan. *Jonathan Swift's Gulliver's Travels.* Ed. Robert A. Greenberg. Rev. ed. New York: Norton, 1978.

Tinker, Grant, with Bud Rukeyser. *Tinker in Television: From General Sarnoff to General Electric.* New York: Simon and Schuster, 1994.

Twitchell, James. *Carnival Culture: The Trashing of Taste in America.* New York: Columbia University Press, 1992.

Ulmer, Gregory L. "The Object of Post-Criticism." In *The Anti-Aesthetic: Essays on Postmodern Culture,* ed. Hal Foster, pp. 83–110. Seattle: Bay Press, 1983.

Venturi, Robert, Denise Scott Brown, and Steven Izenour. *Learning from Las Vegas.* Rev. ed. Cambridge: MIT Press, 1994. Originally published 1972.

Warshow, Robert. "The Gangster as Tragic Hero." In *The Immediate Experience: Movies, Comics, Theatre, and Other Aspects of Popular Culture,* pp. 127–33. Garden City: Doubleday, 1962.

Webster, John. *Three Plays.* London: Penguin, 1972.

Wellek, René. *The Attack on Literature and Other Essays.* Chapel Hill: University of North Carolina Press, 1982.

Wharton, Edith. *The House of Mirth.* New York: Penguin, 1985.

Whyte, William H. *The Organization Man*. New York: Simon and Schuster, 1956.

Williams, Raymond. *Modern Tragedy*. Stanford, Calif.: Stanford University Press, 1966.

Williams, Tennessee. *A Streetcar Named Desire*. New York: New Directions, 1947.

Index

Designer:	Nicole Hayward
Compositor:	Binghamton Valley Composition
Jacket:	Southeastern Printing
Printer and Binder:	Maple-Vail